T0131767

RADICALLY LEGAL

Right in the middle of the German constitution, a group of ordinary citizens discovers a forgotten clause that allows them to take 240,000 homes back from multi-billion corporations. In this work of creative non-fiction, scholar-activist and Nine Dots Prize winner Joanna Kusiak tells the story of a grassroots movement that convinced a million Berliners to pop the speculative housing bubble. She offers a vision of urban housing as democratically held commons, legally managed by a radically new institutional model that works through democratic conflicts. Moving between interdisciplinary analysis and the personal story of her becoming a scholar-activist, Kusiak connects the dots between history and presence, the local and the global, and shows the potential of radically legal politics as a means of strengthening our democracies and reviving the rule of law. This title is also available as Open Access on Cambridge Core.

Joanna Kusiak is a Junior Research Fellow at King's College, University of Cambridge. Her work focuses on urban land, housing crises and the progressive potential of the law. In 2021 she was one of the spokespeople for Deutsche Wohnen & Co. enteignen, Berlin's successful referendum campaign to expropriate stock-listed landlords. In 2023 she won the Nine Dots Prize.

Radically Legal

Berlin Constitutes the Future

JOANNA KUSIAK
University of Cambridge

CAMBRIDGE
UNIVERSITY PRESS

CAMBRIDGE
UNIVERSITY PRESS

Shaftesbury Road, Cambridge CB2 8EA, United Kingdom

One Liberty Plaza, 20th Floor, New York, NY 10006, USA

477 Williamstown Road, Port Melbourne, VIC 3207, Australia

314–321, 3rd Floor, Plot 3, Splendor Forum, Jasola District Centre, New Delhi – 110025, India

103 Penang Road, #05-06/07, Visioncrest Commercial, Singapore 238467

Cambridge University Press is part of Cambridge University Press & Assessment, a department of the University of Cambridge.

We share the University's mission to contribute to society through the pursuit of education, learning and research at the highest international levels of excellence.

www.cambridge.org
Information on this title: www.cambridge.org/9781009516938

DOI: 10.1017/9781009516914

This book is based on research project funded by Poland's National Science Center, grant agreement no. 2019/35/D/HS6/03880. Joanna Kusiak's research in Berlin has also been supported by the Humboldt Foundation and by King's College, Cambridge.

First published 2024

A catalogue record for this publication is available from the British Library.

A Cataloging-in-Publication data record for this book is available from the Library of Congress

ISBN 978-1-009-51693-8 Hardback
ISBN 978-1-009-51694-5 Paperback

To Lisa, my brilliant friend, and to Berlin, the city that brought us together.

Land, natural resources and means of production may, for the purpose of socialisation (*Vergesellschaftung*), be transferred to public ownership (*Gemeineigentum*), or other forms of solidarity economy (*Gemeinwirtschaft*) by a law that determines the nature and extent of compensation.

Article 15, *Grundgesetz für die Bundesrepublik Deutschland*

CONTENTS

FIGURES

ABOUT THE NINE DOTS PRIZE

There is no other literary accolade quite like the Nine Dots Prize. It is anonymously judged, for one, and, just as significantly, it is awarded for a book that does not yet exist.

Every two years its Board convenes to decide on a question inspired by a problem or concern of contemporary global importance. We invite writers from all over the world, whether established or aspiring, to respond to that question in no more than 3,000 words. The most compelling response is awarded $100,000, a book deal from Cambridge University Press, and support from the team at the Centre for Research in the Arts, Social Sciences and Humanities (CRASSH) at Cambridge University. The winning applicant therefore has everything they need to develop their idea into a full-length book which is subsequently sold in bookshops and, crucially, made available online for free.

That the Prize is judged anonymously means each applicant can be confident they are judged purely on the merits of their writing and ideas, and not their CV, background or identity. This is essential if we are to realise our ambition of finding and championing the most exciting thinkers in the world.

In 2022, for our fourth cycle, we posed the question 'Why has the rule of law become so fragile?' Of the hundreds of submissions we received, there emerged a clear frontrunner. Taking the case of the 2021 Berlin Referendum, in which voters decided to expropriate hundreds of thousands of properties from corporate landlords into public ownership, this was an entry that mixed the urgency of contemporary politics with the complexity of recent history. This combination succeeded in winning over our judges. The resulting book is *Radically Legal*, in which Dr Joanna Kusiak deploys both her knowledge and experience as a 'scholar-activist' to demonstrate the potential of this new form of politics to deepen our democracies, renew the rule of law and bring about progressive change.

Joanna Kusiak joins an impressive network of winners, in tech strategist turned Oxford philosopher James Williams, writer and journalist Annie Zaidi, and the journalist Trish Lorenz. We hope that this book will succeed in having a similar impact as those of Kusiak's predecessors, provoking debate, sparking hope and contributing in some part to positive change in our societies.

Professor Simon Goldhill
Professor of Greek Literature and Culture and Fellow of King's College,
Cambridge and Chair of the Nine Dots Prize Board

For more about the Nine Dots Prize, please visit: ninedots-prize.org

Figure 0.1 Deutsche Wohnen & Co. enteignen's cheerleading squad
dancing in front of the Reichstag
(*Source:* Christian Mang)

Figure 1.1 Berlin S-bahn driver giving his signature in support of DWE's referendum
(*Source:* Rory Grubb)

It always seems impossible until it's done.
Nelson Mandela, a peaceful revolutionary

Only we take you exactly as you are.
Berlin Public Transport Company (BVG)

TAKING THE TRAM HOME

Prelude to Change

It was an impulse. Henryka Krzywonos was still hesitating when she saw her hand reach out and press the brake. 'Ladies and gentlemen,' she shouted, at the top of her voice, 'This tram is not going any further!' She feared the passengers would lynch her, but Tram 15 burst into applause! Following her lead, two buses stopped in the opposite lane. It was 15 August 1980. The Regional Transport Company had joined a wave of strikes that were rolling across Poland in response to the rising costs of living – and the political repression of the strikers.

The authorities cut the phone lines to disable communication between the striking companies. And so, the next morning, Henryka Krzywonos showed up in person at the Gdańsk shipyard – one of the most powerful centres of the strikes – to share her news. To her dismay, she learned that, just as the Regional Transport Company was joining the strike, the shipyard workers had decided to end theirs. The management of the shipyard had met its workers' demands.

But Henryka Krzywonos couldn't take this news back to her colleagues at the tram depot. Everyone was counting on the shipyard's support! Furious, she leapt up onto a forklift truck. 'You mustn't end the strike now!' she yelled. 'The authorities won't take on the shipyard, because it has power – but we can't cope on our own! My trams can't take on their tanks! They'll squash us like insects!' A man with a moustache walked up to her. His name was Lech Wałęsa. 'All right,' he said. 'We'll make this a solidarity strike.' And that was how Solidarność began: a social movement that overthrew authoritarian communism in Poland and cracked the Eastern Bloc open.

Clutching your coffee in the usual weather, you wait sleepily at your tram stop for the everyday repetition of everything. One day – maybe it is drizzling – a tram of history arrives. It is never the case that *everyone* jumps aboard. Some people hate mass transit and would only ever travel by car. Others are used to walking in the drizzle. But this is the magic of democracy as a means of public transport: if enough people get on board, everyone is taken to the future (Figure 1.1).

I remember waiting, excited, at the Danziger Strasse tram stop in Berlin. It was a sunny Sunday. On 26 September 2021, the city shimmered in the Indian summer – and 1 million people decided to take €36 billion worth of housing away from big finance. A total of 59.1 per cent of Berliners voted 'Yes!' in a referendum to expropriate more than 240,000 apartments owned by stock-listed, multi-billion-euro corporations. Most of these apartments were once publicly owned; they were privatised for knockdown prices in the noughties. Now, Berliners want to 'socialise' them – to turn them into a democratically managed commons.

Imagine this: 240,000 investment properties will be withdrawn from corporate asset portfolios and restored to their primary function: as people's homes. A new public institution will distribute and manage this housing in a democratic way, catering to the needs of all Berliners, not just the current tenants. The city will compensate the corporations for their property, but at well below current market prices. The rents must be affordable.

Expropriating multi-billion corporations might sound like a revolution – but no one is storming the Reichstag. The social movement Deutsche Wohnen & Co. enteignen (DWE) won the referendum by following established democratic procedures. The 1 million YES! votes for socialisation came from across the political spectrum. The weapon with which Berliners will expropriate the stock-listed corporations is peaceful but powerful. It's the German Constitution – *das Grundgesetz*.

This revolution is radically legal. It is powered by the law. Etymologically, 'radical' means 'proceeding from the roots', and DWE is challenging global financial capital by going back to the roots of Germany's legal system. Among the fundamental rights laid out in the *Grundgesetz* there lies a forgotten clause: Article 15. It allows land, natural resources and means of production to

be expropriated and turned into public property for the purpose
of 'socialisation' (*Vergesellschaftung*).

The constitutional purpose of socialisation is to foster
Gemeinwirtschaft – a form of economic enterprise (or an entire
system) that prioritises social good over financial profits, and is
governed in a democratic way. *Gemeinwirtschaft* is closest to the
English term 'solidarity economy'.[1] However, *Gemeinwirtschaft*
has a much longer tradition: together with socialisation
(*Vergesellschaftung*), it is part of the legacy of the German
Revolution of 1918–19.[2]

Socialisation and *Gemeinwirtschaft* were first introduced as
legal concepts by the Weimar Constitution. From there, they
made it into the *Grundgesetz*. After the Second World War,
socialisation was considered an important tool to prevent a
'misuse of economic power' against democracy – as happened
when industrial monopolists funded Hitler's project of destroying the trade unions. With *Gemeinwirtschaft*, conservative and
socialist parties alike expressed their aspiration to democratise
the economy. However, after the German 'economic miracle' of
the 1950s, *Gemeinwirtschaft* was largely forgotten. So was Article
15: no government ever based any legislation on it.

The roaring 'Yes!' of those 1 million Berliners awakened the
right to socialisation from its decades-long slumber in the safe
folds of the *Grundgesetz*. Berliners have asked the law to constitute a future in which everyone can afford to live. Legally, such a
future is possible. But is it possible in reality?

Of course not. A system in which housing is beautiful, ecologically sustainable and universally affordable is utterly impossible … just as women's rights were once 'impossible', or taking
down the Berlin Wall. The purpose of the 2021 referendum was
to stop the tram from proceeding along its customary route of
ever-increasing rents. But even as Berliners pull the lever to
switch the tracks towards *Gemeinwirtschaft*, powerful people are
trying to stop them. They want to return the tram to an old
depot with 'there is no alternative' written above its gates.
Do not underestimate them. These people only like democracy
until they realise it is a means of public transport.

In the popular imagination, revolutions are sharp turns of history. Events flip from the impossible to the inevitable, bypassing the improbable. These accounts underestimate the courage and persistence necessary in order to enact change. When Henryka Krzywonos pressed the brake on her tram, she wasn't planning to bring about the collapse of the Eastern Bloc. She listened to her inner sense of justice, and implemented her freedom. And the shipyard workers, though satisfied with their own success, did not dismiss her anger. They saw it for what it was: a call for solidarity. Between stopping the tram in Gdańsk and the start of Polish democracy there lies a decade of work by Solidarność, with medium-sized victories and major defeats along the way. Even now, Solidarność's democratic revolution remains unfinished. And your democracy? Is it already *democratic enough*?

The tram of history has left the Berlin depot with 1 million people on board. It is heading towards the future – but many different levers may still be pulled along the way. Each chapter of this book is like a stop that the tram has already passed, or that is coming into view on the horizon. After jumping on the tram here, at Tram Stop One, you'll be joined by other Berliners at the stops that follow, and will get to know the city.

At Tram Stop Two, you will find out why the tram is setting out from Berlin, and why now. Immanuel Kant appears on a horse at the Constitutional Court to explain why property is important for freedom. The Berlin housing system functioned as practically as German chocolate, and provided people with homes. Suddenly, a choir announces the arrival of the corporate landlords. Like the Jabberwock, these corporations only exist as fictions – which gives them real power.

At Tram Stop Three, the fictional Jabberwock is haunted by real ghosts. Dressed up in bedsheets, these spectres of expropriation are ordinary, hard-working people. They use the law to push the boundaries of what is politically possible. Albert Einstein supports them, but the lobbyists push back. DWE wins the referendum, but has to prepare for another one.

Departing from Tram Stop Four, we take a detour through history. The tram speeds like a rollercoaster through the past.

Hitler is fundraising. The Parliamentary Council writes the *Grundgesetz*, obsessing about checks and balances. Article 15 turns out to be less controversial than gender equality. In a century-defining boxing match between a conservative and a social-democratic jurist, globalisation declares itself the winner. Democracy loses against debt. All state power derives from the people, but the people struggle with impostor syndrome.

At Tram Stop Five, things get curiouser and curiouser. A Berliner takes us into a future that was notably absent from the FUTURE PropTech conference in London. Bruno Taut pioneers palpable utopias, and a centenarian writes a book in the hope of saving them. With Kant's horse and David Bowie on board, the tram arrives at a sexy new institution that manages socialised housing and democratic disputes. At last you can relax with a glass of wine – and legislate well-balanced compensation for the expropriated corporations.

At Tram Stop Six, the rule of law is having a midlife crisis. A Berlin judge plans to storm the Reichstag, riding on a cloud of free-floating rage. All the skeletons tumble out of the closet: it turns out that everyone has *feelings*. Democracy embraces difference, and engenders conflict. In an effort to stay rational, DWE activists explore their anger and write a law. The sponsor of the Nine Dots Prize realises that his Berlin assets might be affected, and mulls over a plan to stop my ideas from spreading.

In the Epilogue – Tram Stop Seven – a Berghain bouncer opens the gates of the law to Franz Kafka. Kafka's K. meets other letters of the alphabet, and joins DWE's cheerleading team outside the Reichstag.

The events described in this book are brought to you by the number 15, and by a whole alphabet of letters. Both the iconic Solidarność tram and the constitutional article that makes socialisation possible bear the number 15. Maybe 15 is democracy's lucky number. The DWE activists who appear in this book have asked to be represented only by their initials. This is because, while all are equally important, it is simply not possible to name all the activists involved: over time, more than 3,000 people have contributed directly to the movement. Their individual contributions may differ in character and quantity, but democracy needs all of us: an alphabet of people who write the future by repeatedly coming together.

In writing this book about the DWE alphabet, I hold a double position: I am the author, and I am one of the letters. I am a scholar-activist. I am an urban sociologist at the University of Cambridge, and I have spent the last decade researching the ways in which democratic movements use the law to bring about radical social change. I joined Deutsche Wohnen & Co. enteignen in 2019; before that, I worked with housing movements in Warsaw. My research topic was not an accidental choice. I, too, once struggled to find an affordable home.

I am a Berliner – but the story of how I became a Berliner begins in Poland, with Solidarność. Over the course of this book, I will show you how I have travelled from one story to another: jumping on the tram of history, hoping it will take me home.

②

Figure 2.1 Socialisation: Lawful, affordable, good. A pastiche of Ritter Sport advertisement created by Joanna Kusiak as part of the public art exhibition *Die Balkone* in Berlin Prenzlauer Berg, 2021 (*Source:* Joanna Kusiak)

All free men, wherever they may live, are citizens of Berlin and, therefore, as a free man, I take pride in the words 'Ich bin ein Berliner.'
John F. Kennedy, President of the United States, and for one day also a Berliner

What's picking a lock compared to buying shares?
Bertolt Brecht, Berliner, Playwright

WE ARE ALL STAYING PUT

Property and Freedom

1

Because Herr Meier was yelling, I couldn't understand his exact words. Frau Tams, on the other hand, was speaking with soft confidence, folding words I understood perfectly into sentences that sounded baroquely mysterious. But sometimes we get to *feel* the implications of what is happening long before we grasp it in words. That scorching summer, in a cool chamber of the administrative court in Berlin-Mitte, Herr Meier and I had both arrived at the same truth, one that neither of us had really *felt* before: that I, too, was free.

'A student from Poland is not going to tell me what I can or cannot do with my property!' Herr Meier had told me, a few weeks earlier. I had challenged his rent increase, and he had threatened to terminate my contract. When I saw him at his office, with an oil-on-canvas painting of a red sports car right behind his head, I sensed that he took his power advantage for granted. Now, in court, his face was contorted in a furious grimace. I had written my master's thesis on Walter Benjamin in Herr Meier's apartment, and it suddenly occurred to me that my landlord must be experiencing what Benjamin called 'the mythical violence of the law'.[1] In his defence, he kept repeating the word *Eigentümer*, owner. Herr Meier was the owner. And who was I?

Amid the strange music of German legal jargon, I felt the mythical violence of the law burning new pathways through my identity. It was as if Frau Tams, a lawyer from the Berlin Tenants' Association, were casting spells on me. With her first spell she turned a poor student into a legal subject. With her second spell she turned a Polish migrant into a rightful Berliner. For her third spell, Frau Tams said nothing: she left me in a space where I could turn myself into whatever I wanted to be. Because I was free. That scorching summer, the law completed in me a new notion of freedom. After years of just being free to go, Berlin had made me free to stay.

2

I have property rights in Herr Meier's apartment; and I am still here, writing these words in another hot Berlin summer, feeling the cool wooden floor of my home beneath my feet. It has been seventeen years since I first moved in, and nearly seven since the last of the four court cases I brought against my landlord, all of which I won. I do not fully grasp Germany's complex tenant protection laws (*Mietrecht*), but this I have understood: as a tenant, I have property rights in my home.

Naturally, Herr Meier remains the *Eigentümer*, the property owner. He is free to sell the whole building, cashing in on its current market value. And he was free to sign the rental agreement with me. But he cannot change the terms of our contract by raising the rent excessively, nor can he terminate it without valid legal grounds. As long as I dutifully pay the rent we agreed, I am a lawful *Besitzerin*, a property holder. This, too, is a form of ownership – the law says that I exercise 'actual control' (*tatsächliche Herrschaft*)[2] over the apartment. This is my home, and Herr Meier cannot enter it without making an appointment with me. Since our last lawsuit, Herr Meier and I have learned to coexist in peace. I accept his freedom, and he accepts mine.

My property rights in Herr Meier's apartment are, like his property rights, protected by the German constitution, the *Grundgesetz*. In May 1993, the Federal Constitutional Court (*Bundesverfassungsgericht*) decided that the rights of a tenant as a property holder count as property rights, because they fulfil the purpose of the fundamental right (*Grundrecht*) to property.[3] The fundamental right to property has a broader meaning than the title of ownership as defined by the Civil Code. The *Grundgesetz* protects property as a moral concept, a positive right upholding human dignity and freedom.

In Germany, as soon as a discussion starts about morality or freedom, you'll hear the clip-clopping of hooves as Immanuel Kant comes galloping into the debate on his great Holsteiner horse.

'Now I say,' Kant asserts, in one of the formulations of his 'categorical imperative', 'that the human being … *exists* as an end in itself, *not merely as a means* to be used by this or that will at its discretion; instead he must in all his actions, whether directed to himself or also to other rational beings, always be regarded *at the same time as an end*'.[4]

Rooted in Kantian ethics, the whole *Grundgesetz* can be seen as an attempt to translate categorical imperative into public law. That's why, unlike in the American tradition, all constitutional rights come with constitutional duties.[5] Article 1 declares that human dignity shall be inviolable, and that it is the duty of all state authority to protect it. Article 2 follows with the inviolability of freedom, and states that 'every person shall have the right to free development of their personality insofar as they do not violate the rights of others'.[6] The right to personality, also inspired by Kant, protects a person's intellectual and spiritual integrity. It assumes that, to become fully human, we need both the possibility of acting in the world and a protected sphere of privacy to which we may withdraw.[7] To be free means to be capable of acting like a free moral agent – a capacity that should be restricted neither by an external force nor by dire existential need.

To enable such moral freedom, further down the line Article 14 guarantees the right to property. Remarkably, though, all three clauses of the Article intended to protect property also imply its limitation. The first clause states that the contents and limits of property guarantees shall be defined by law, implying that they are not absolute. The second clause declares that property entails obligations, and that its use shall also serve the public good. The final clause allows for expropriation in the interest of the public good.

Coming from the Kantian tradition, the limitations of property seem logical: property is a positive right, created within the context of a society and subordinated to its needs. But when you mention the limitations of property to people in England, or in the United States, moral panic ensues. Can someone please call in John Locke? Locke is to the Anglo-Saxons what Kant is to the Germans: the main philosopher theorising property and freedom. According to Locke, property is a result of mixing things with labour. This argument is foundational for Western liberalism, and is often used to justify the unlimited accumulation of property.

Here comes Locke, riding in on his English Thoroughbred. Called to defend unlimited property rights, he throws up his hands. In *Two Treatises of Government*, he set three clear restrictions on the accumulation of property: you can only accumulate as much as you can use before it spoils; you must leave 'enough and as good' for others; and you can only appropriate property through your own labour.[8] That's the trouble with writing books – you cudgel your brain to figure out the complexity, and people only remember what's convenient.

The Federal Constitutional Court remains true to Kant. In Germany, it was the Kantian right to freedom, not social welfare rights, that gave tenants property rights in the 1993 ruling. The Court noted that an apartment in which a person lives is 'the spatial centre of free development of their personality' and a person's 'free space of independent activity'.[9] It thus possesses the constitutional attributes of property, regardless of the title of ownership. If the property rights of a tenant collide with those of a landlord, they must be measured against each other: which have a more relevant impact on the personal freedom of the rights holder?

The right to property as a home is deemed more relevant for personal freedom than the right to property as a means for gaining wealth. The owner's *Eigenbedarf* – the right to make direct personal use of one's property – always trumps tenant rights: 'The landlord is protected in his freedom to use the dwelling again himself as his centre of life (or to have it used by privileged relatives) in case of his own need.'[10] However, a tenant cannot be uprooted simply because it would bring the landlord more money. A tenant must be treated not as a means of profit, but as a full human – dignified and free.

3

I was not born free to go – but I was raised to go for freedom. I was born in Poland in 1985, at the midpoint of the dramatic arc of the Solidarność movement. In August 1980, workers hung two wooden boards with twenty-one demands at the entrance to the Gdańsk shipyard. They wanted freedom of speech and association, and the release of political prisoners. They also demanded salary increases, paid maternity leave and better access to housing. After more than two weeks of intense strikes and negotiations, Solidarność was launched as the first free trade union in communist Poland. Soon, its membership had increased to 10 million – a third of Poland's working population.

By 1981, Solidarność was one of the biggest social movements in the history of the world. Its programme was deeply democratic, combining political liberties with economic self-governance. Alarmed by this vision, the authoritarian government took away people's freedom. In December 1981, tanks rolled onto the streets as the government introduced martial law, de-legalising Solidarność and imprisoning its activists. A mere eight years later, Solidarność won a landslide victory in Poland's first democratic elections. At the time, I was just learning to read, focusing on the big fonts of the newspaper headlines. *WOLNOŚĆ* – freedom – was everywhere, and it became a basic tenet of my childhood that people can move the immovable by becoming a movement.

The two things I remember most vividly from the early period of Poland's new freedom are: a TV commercial for a global brand of scouring cream ('cleans effectively, doesn't scratch'); and the screams that echoed around my prefab estate after dark. The commercials, played before the evening cartoons, were a beacon of the new reality. The adults interrupted their household chores to watch them with us – shiny promises of a capitalist world so abundant that even our stoves could feel safe. The screams in the dark outside my window suggested that the reality was actually far scarier. In Łódź, the working-class city where I grew up that was soon to be dubbed 'the Polish Detroit', violence spiked with the collapse of the textile industry. This collapse was triggered by neoliberal shock therapy, an economic programme first tested by Pinochet in Chile and legally adopted in Poland on the day of my fourth birthday.

Unlike the scouring cream, the shock therapy had to be abrasive in order to be efficient.[11] That, at least, was the opinion of the economic experts who ordained it. With a triple blow of privatisation, deregulation and austerity, the shock therapy brought in international investors while removing social safety nets; it opened up lucrative business opportunities while creating unemployment and hyperinflation. In its efficiency, it quickly divided Poles into 'winners' and 'losers' of the transformation.[12] My family landed in between. My mother was a widowed teacher; unlike industrial workers, she didn't lose her job, but her salary was constantly losing value. The mixture of austerity and hyperinflation turned us into a social class that is common in eastern Europe, but confusing for Western Europeans: the educated poor.

The new system told us it was our freedom and responsibility to become who we were meant to be – winners, or losers. Ambitious as I was, at age 18 I became both. In May 2004, I won the silver medal at the International Philosophy Olympiad in Seoul – a global essay competition for gifted high-school students – and was accepted on an elite liberal arts study programme at the University of Warsaw. Six months later, walking the streets of Warsaw, I felt I had no home. Without money or social networks, all I could afford on the 'free' housing market was a tiny room with a barred window in a grumpy old lady's apartment. I had no rights, and no formal contract. My landlady rummaged through my things, and strictly timed my showers.

I received scholarships for academic excellence, but they were not enough to cover standard Warsaw rents. The private rental market was 'free', while scholarships at a public university were subject to austerity. Realising that I was struggling, some of my well-meaning professors felt compelled to offer advice. One urged me simply to buy a flat. He suggested that I take out a mortgage in Swiss francs to save money. This was a popular option in eastern Europe at the time, promoted by financial experts as a clever way of saving on interest rates. My family was too poor to take out a mortgage, which turned out to be a blessing in disguise. Years later, I would describe the bursting of the Swiss franc mortgage bubble in my PhD thesis.

Meanwhile, another professor who appreciated my research skills found me a job: analysing press reports about a corruption scandal involving prominent Solidarność figures and Warsaw real estate. I quickly realised that it included the land beneath the luxury apartment (the office space provided by my employers) I was sitting in, conducting the analysis. My employers were friends of my professor, and of the freshly imprisoned protagonist of the scandal. They hired me privately to try to make sense of what had happened. The salary was decent and, combined with the scholarship, it meant that I finally had enough money to rent a small place overlooking a six-lane highway.

And then I left. I was offered a scholarship in Berlin to conduct research for my master's thesis on Walter Benjamin. The stipend was offered by an eastern European institution, and by German standards it was rather low. But so was my Berlin rent. For the first time in my life, I didn't need to work double shifts, and could focus on studying and writing. I was only supposed to stay six months, but my rental contract was open-ended. I felt too free to give it up, so I stayed in Berlin.

I wasn't the only one to stay. Poles are the second largest migrant population in Berlin. The older generation tells stories of escaping the constraints of communism for the freedom of democracy. We, the millennial migrants, arrive freely and en masse. Once here, we often realise that we, too, have escaped. We've escaped the cut-throat struggle of neoliberal austerity for the freedom of *social* democracy.

On my first day as a Berliner, I dropped my suitcase in the hall and went for a walk. Just five minutes later, I found myself in the middle of Bruno Taut's Carl Legien Estate, a stunning example of 1920s modernism. I was so hungry for the Berlin experience that I dwelled on every little detail. I peeked into the windows of a ground-floor apartment, and checked what was growing in the allotment gardens in a green courtyard. I tailgated an old lady through the Bauhaus-style entrance, just to smell the staircase.

I tested my German on the little announcement sheet: *This estate has been acquired by Deutsche Wohnen*. It was 2007. The housing crisis from which I had just found refuge was following me to Berlin. Back then, though, I didn't know that. I took some photos of the stunning Bauhaus vistas (Figure 2.2) and went home.

Figure 2.2 Bruno Taut's Carl Legien Estate in Berlin Prenzlauer Berg (*Source:* Karsten Buch)

4

One cultural phenomenon that really struck me during my first year in Germany was an advert for chocolate. Ritter Sport has been using the same, familiar slogan since the 1970s: 'Square. Practical. Good.' (*Quadratisch. Praktisch. Gut.*). The chocolate is indeed square-shaped; this was a breakthrough invention by the company's founder in 1932. Clara Ritter wanted to create a more practical, standard-weight chocolate bar that would fit neatly into everyone's pocket. Her square chocolate bar is patented, along with its practical wrapper, which you can open simply by breaking the bar in half. Ritter Sport has remained one of Germany's bestselling products for almost a century.

I was stunned. I didn't know any other culture that would advertise chocolate as *practical*. The chocolate ads I was familiar with would either romanticise the sweetness of childhood or lure their target audience with the promise of more adult pleasures, images of silky-smooth chocolate slowly melting behind full, feminine lips. I realised that what Germans sought in their chocolate was the ultimate delight of ... functionality.

It made sense. Ritter Sport is the chocolate equivalent of Bauhaus – not only because of its geometry. Both Bauhaus and Ritter Sport strive for universality; their functionality pledges to work for everyone. They do not over-promise, or aspire to being 'incredible'. All they want is to be credibly good. Their beauty is humble, and stems from quality rather than seduction. Part of their goodness is the fact that everyone can afford a piece of it. It's not Belgian truffles or Italian palazzos: it's German functionalism at its best.

The German propensity for functionalism permeates the entire culture. An important part of it is the willingness to think of issues in terms of 'systems', even if not all their elements have been designed together in a conscious or purposeful way. The housing system is an excellent example. It wasn't 'designed' in one go, but was negotiated over time to accommodate the social, political and economic functions housing was expected to fulfil.

The social functions of housing were recognised in the nineteenth century. Germany's tenant protection laws date back to the Kingdom of Prussia. These rights were progressively strengthened to overcome the acute housing shortages after the First and Second World Wars. To ensure that everyone had fair access to housing, local authorities were legally empowered to control its allocation. Consecutive governments legislated for a rent cap, introduced new measures to prevent discrimination in the housing market, and restricted the valid reasons for eviction. Many of these regulations are still in place today.

Politically, the German republic expects the housing system to fulfil both the liberal ideal of freedom and the conservative ideal of rootedness. Both require stability, guaranteed either by private ownership or by tenant protections. 'What is necessary for freedom is not wealth,' Hannah Arendt once stressed. 'What is necessary is security and a place of one's own shielded from the claims of the public.'[13] So it's not just Kant: philosophical tradition abounds in arguments about property being a necessary condition for freedom and democracy. What is unique about the German rule of law, however, is that it assumes the state is responsible for providing *access* to (housing) property, even as it also maintains the unequal distribution of property ownership.

Finally, affordable housing was always functionally important for the German economy. Broad access to affordable housing was a strategic element of West Germany's post-war 'economic miracle' (*Wirtschaftswunder*). Because rent is a major expense in household budgets, keeping rents low made it possible to keep salaries low without risking social unrest. This, in turn, lowered the cost of production, boosting Germany's export capacity. That's why, even in 'capitalist' West Berlin, most new housing was either built by public and non-profit institutions, or had strictly regulated 'social' rents.

Over the course of history, all of these different functions of housing were being inscribed in law. Of course, even with the best laws there can be no guarantee that they will be enforced. The idea that we are all equal before the law turns out to be an illusion when we are confronted with structural imbalances of power.[14] To counter this imbalance, as early as 1888, Berlin tenants organised themselves into the Berliner Mieterverein, a legally oriented association that effectively functions as a tenant union, lobbying for better regulations and ensuring that the existing ones are enforced. Around 250,000 Berlin households are members of one of the three existing unions.[15]

Tenant unions are a game changer because of the legal protection insurance included in the modest membership fee. If a conflict between a tenant and a landlord cannot be resolved without litigation, the union provides a lawyer, and the insurance covers all the costs incurred. In this way, the union empowers people to seek justice in courts – people who could never otherwise afford to do so, or have other reasons for balking at the prospect of a lawsuit: because they are migrants, for example, or lack knowledge, or have experienced discrimination. I, too, would never have dared to sue Herr Meier had I not had the assistance of Frau Tams, the impressively capable union lawyer, and the certainty that I would not end up in debt even if I lost. With the union behind me, losing seemed less damaging than not trying to win.

The Berlin housing system was forged in the process of political, social and legal negotiations about the different functions it had to fulfil. There was plenty of room for improvement, but also enough room for the people. Just like the popular chocolate, Berlin's housing system squared different expectations to fit the common pocket. It wasn't perfect – no system is – but it was reliably good. It functioned.

5

When the system stopped functioning, people tried different strategies. One Saturday in 2015, a whole choir squeezed into the elevator of a building in Kreuzberg.

'*Guten Tag*, you are connected with the maintenance service of Deutsche Wohnen,' the choir intoned, like a priest chanting. 'All our lines are busy at the moment … If your name is Ahmed or

Hatice, or if your income is low for any other reason, press one ... If you have a complaint, please deal with it yourself. Please hang up. Please give up. Please press one and we will terminate your contract as soon as possible.'[16]

The building they sang in was near Kotti, which is what Berliners call the area around the Kottbusser Tor subway station. The municipal non-profit housing company that built it, GSW, was privatised in 2004. In 2013, it was acquired by Deutsche Wohnen. Soon, Deutsche Wohnen had become a paradigmatic example of Berlin's new type of landlord: the stock-listed corporation.

From the perspective of tenants, the system stopped functioning when the corporate landlords arrived. They could literally feel it. The heating broke down in the middle of January, when temperatures in Berlin were around minus six Celsius. No one came to repair it for more than three weeks. The *Hausmeister*, the caretaker responsible for building maintenance, had been replaced by a call centre, where an automated voice provided zero assistance to the accompaniment of a synthesised tune. At the same time, tenants were also receiving letters about impending rent increases.

From the perspective of Deutsche Wohnen, the system was functioning splendidly. Their stock prices kept on rising. In their annual reports, corporate managers proudly highlighted their successes in implementing ever-new 'measures with rent-increasing potential', by which they meant cutting maintenance and terminating rental contracts prematurely. The latter strategy could be especially profitable: it allowed the landlords to 'unlock the reversionary potential' and raise rents by up to 30 per cent, which translated to an increase in shareholders' dividend payments.[17]

Crucial to unlocking this potential was Deutsche Wohnen's legal department. A team of well-paid corporate lawyers was tasked with removing any legal obstacles to increasing rents, or else finding loopholes in existing regulations. One such loophole involves raising the rent on the grounds of ecological modernisation. This led to frustrating situations in which Deutsche Wohnen would 'modernise' a building's insulation to justify a rent increase, but would not repair faulty heating or remove mould – this is legally classified as 'maintenance', and cannot be cited as the grounds for a rent increase.

As well as raising rents for individual tenants, Deutsche Wohnen's lawyers also launched a full-frontal attack on the existing regulations. In 2017, the corporation filed a lawsuit aimed at invalidating the 'rent mirror' (*Mietspiegel*), a benchmark introduced in 1974 to establish upper rent limits based on the average rent in a given area. As it owned more than 115,000 apartments in Berlin, Deutsche Wohnen was also driving up the benchmark by increasing rents in its own housing stock.[18] Its tenants sought help from the tenant unions, but with an army of corporate lawyers against them, the union lawyers were permanently on the defensive.

The effects of the corporate rent-increase offensive have gradually spilled over to affect the whole system. While Deutsche Wohnen was the biggest of the corporate landlords, with a market share of around 6 per cent, several other corporate landlords were using similar strategies: Vonovia, ADO Properties, Covivio, Akelius, Grand Properties, Heimstaden, Adler Group and Pears International. Together, they owned at least 240,000 apartments in the city. By 2018, Berlin – which used to be one of the most affordable capital cities in Europe – was the world number one 'city with the fastest-rising property prices', with a 20.5 per cent price increase in just one year.

Why did the stock-listed landlords decide to dismantle the housing system that had been balancing people's needs against other functions of urban housing for more than a century? Couldn't corporations somehow adapt to the system? No, they could not – because although corporate landlords operate *within* the Berlin housing system, structurally they belong to a completely different system: the global financial system.

These two systems cater to very different, even opposing functions. The purpose of the Berlin housing system has been to provide housing to Berliners, while also supporting the political and economic functioning of the city. Its legal regulations, inscribed in public administrative law, were conceived to uphold these functions. A stock-listed corporation, on the other hand, is a creature whose existence is governed primarily by corporate law. Its main purpose is to maximise shareholder profit.

As an invention of legal engineering, corporation is as ingenious as the nuclear bomb. This was the opinion of Adolf A. Berle and Gardiner C. Means, the authors of *The Modern Corporation and Private Property*, published in 1932, which remains the most quoted book in corporate governance studies. Although corporation derives its power from concentrating property rights, it can only achieve this by 'blasting the atom of property', purposefully destroying all the links that constitute the liberal understanding of property.

The liberal understanding of property (as inscribed, among others, in the German *Grundgesetz*) sees property as a relationship between a person and a thing (me and my jacket), mediated by a social contract (the state declares it illegal for others to steal my jacket). By fissioning these two relationships, corporation produces 'a centripetal attraction which draws wealth together into aggregations of constantly increasing size, at the same time throwing control into the hands of fewer and fewer men'.[19] This gives it truly 'nuclear' power.

How was it possible to blast the atom of property? In order to achieve this, legal engineers wrapped the concept of property in legal fictions. Inventing 'legal fictions' is a standard legal procedure. For the purposes of legal coherence, the law may establish something as true, even if it is not true in reality.

Corporation is one such legal fiction, because it assumes the corporation to be a person. Literally, incorporation means creating a new *corpus* – a new body. This body is fictional, and fully disembodied. Corporation has neither materiality nor needs; it does not have to eat or sleep. Factually, corporation is a 'nexus of contracts', but – and this is the 'quantum leap in legal engineering'[20] – this 'nexus of contracts' is endowed with some of the rights of a human person, including the right to property.

The purpose of corporate personhood is to break the link between a person and a thing. This makes corporate property unintuitive and hard to understand. Let's take the example of Deutsche Wohnen. We tend to assume that Deutsche Wohnen is owned by its shareholders, and that by owning Deutsche

Wohnen, the shareholders also own the apartments. But legally speaking, none of this is true.

Firstly, no real people own Deutsche Wohnen – not even the shareholders. This is confusing even to experts. While the EU shareholders' rights directive explicitly states that 'shareholders do not own the corporation',[21] a Google search will still direct you to plenty of credible-looking pages suggesting otherwise. Corporate property beats common sense, because we are used to the idea that companies are owned by people who, in this way, also indirectly own the companies' assets. My landlord owns my apartment via a limited liability company (GmbH), which is owned by him. This is different in the case of a corporation: Deutsche Wohnen is equivalent not to Herr Meier's company, but to Herr Meier himself.

Secondly, no real people own Deutsche Wohnen's apartments. The corporation owns the apartments, and the shareholders own the shares. Shares are bundles of contractual obligations: legally enforceable promises of chunks of corporate profits. Isn't owning profits from the apartments effectively a form of owning the apartments? – No. Unlike real owners, shareholders have no right to make decisions about the corporation's assets. They cannot move into an apartment claiming *Eigenbedarf* (the owner's priority of personal use).

Financial property, like shares, is detached from material things. The purpose of owning stock is purely financial gain. The advantages are easy liquidity, low taxation and a lack of duty of care. If you own an apartment, you are responsible for it: you get things repaired and pay land taxes. If you want to sell it, it takes time and effort, and your profits are taxed at relatively high rates. Shares, on the other hand, can be bought and sold in nanoseconds. Also, while a corporation cannot be owned by an actual human, it can be owned by another corporation, which helps avoid taxes.

In 2021, Deutsche Wohnen was bought by Vonovia, another corporate landlord. But what was formally sold were 86.8 per cent of its corporate shares, not any of Deutsche Wohnen's more than 115,000 Berlin apartments. Indirect sales of land are not taxed unless the buyer acquires at least 95 per cent of the shares.

Vonovia was therefore exempt from the taxes a real person would have to pay if they sold so much as a single apartment.

Thirdly, the possibility of avoiding regular taxation is one of the ways in which corporate property fissures the link between the owner and the society in which the assets are embedded. Because corporation is a fictitious persona, corporate property literally belongs to no one. Many shareholders do not even know what assets are hidden behind their shares. In a financialised chain, in which shares in one corporation are owned by another corporation, ownership becomes depersonalised and geographically detached.

This was the main concern of Berle and Means: corporate managers control assets they do not own, while also wielding enormous power over the social context in which those assets materially exist.[22] That was why they pleaded for democratic checks and balances to hold corporate managers accountable. This was in 1932 – and if things have changed since then, they've gone in the opposite direction.

Currently, the most common principle of corporate governance is the maximisation of shareholder value. For that, rather than creating new value in the real world, corporate managers receive huge premiums. This has been criticised even within the corporate world itself. In the words of Jack Welch, the late CEO of General Electric, shareholder value is 'the dumbest idea in the world', because it sacrifices long-term goals for short-term profits.[23]

In corporate lingo, there is a special word for the non-financial results of corporate operations: *externalities*. Externalities do not appear on corporate balance sheets; only profit is deemed relevant and recorded. Corporate law does not oblige corporations to account for externalities: legally, these are 'other people's problems'.[24] In corporate reports, an 80-year-old Frau Müller who is freezing in her apartment, and her neighbour who can no longer afford his rent, are externalities. Neither corporate managers nor shareholders see us – Berliners – as Kantian dignified and free subjects. To them, we are just externalities.

6

Our cities are becoming externalities, too. According to the sociologist Saskia Sassen, the massive corporate buying of urban land after the 2008 financial crisis is altering the historical meaning of the city as a place of diversity. The scale of corporate ownership of cities is unprecedented: already, a single investment fund owns more of London than either the City of London or the King of England.[25] The prioritised function of this land is the extraction of profit.

Urban politics is ultimately land politics. To govern a city is to govern a territory. Cities in Ancient Greece and Rome were open to foreigners, but these foreigners could not own land without special permission. Now, urban land is increasingly owned by abstract legal entities that are socially and spatially detached from the urban community. By owning the urban land, they effectively cogovern our lives, influencing urban politics while remaining sheltered from its impact. This has consequences for both democracy and rights.

Cities were the birthplace of democracy, ancient and modern, because of their openness and diversity. In cities, even relatively powerless people could participate in popular politics and create culture. By virtue of their presence and visibility, they could 'make their powerlessness complex'.[26] Now, as urban land is subordinated to the logic of profit on a mass scale, cities are becoming significantly more closed and homogenous.

Functionally, corporations are profit-extracting machines of enormous power. Given power over urban land, they are legally enabled to sacrifice the social, cultural and political functions of the city to the logic of profit. In London and New York, thousands of homes are deliberately kept empty to increase their value as investment properties.[27] San Francisco and Sydney lack essential workers: teachers, nurses and garbage truck drivers cannot afford the overblown rents. This is no longer 'gentrification': these cities struggle to function.

How has it all happened? Back in 2008, the financial crisis was caused by the speculative housing and mortgage bubble in the

US urban areas. Central banks around the world responded to the crisis with low-interest-rate policies and 'quantitative easing', injecting extra money into the financial system to encourage borrowing and spending. Suddenly, the financial elites responsible for the crisis had lots of cheap money to spend once more. They sent out their emissaries – stock-listed corporations and investment funds – to scan the globe in search of new opportunities, and soon they descended on cities.

'Why are these houses so cheap?', a London client asked a Berlin real estate broker in 2014. 'Are they radioactive?' The broker laughs as he tells this story to Andreas Wilcke, the director of the documentary *City as Prey*.[28] When corporate capital discovered Berlin, its housing – kept purposefully affordable for decades by the regulations of the system – cost an eighth, or even a tenth, of the London equivalent. Later in the film, we see the same broker with another client, who points at a building in the Berlin district of Friedrichshain and asks how long it would take to modernise it, in order to raise the rents. 'You know, first of all you must have an idea how to take out all the tenants,' the broker replies, in slightly halting English.

In this respect, corporate landlords had an immediate advantage over individual ones: their legal departments had more and bolder ideas about how to 'take out all the tenants' or get around the regulations. For them, Berlin was just a collection of assets that, because of the democratically negotiated regulations, were 'under-priced'. If only these regulations could be lifted or circumvented, the assets would catch up with global prices. From this perspective, Berlin looked like an El Dorado for investors. Furthermore, the city's own politicians proceeded to put this El Dorado on discount sale.

Before the 2008 global financial crisis, Berlin had its own real-estate financial crisis in 2001: the 'Berlin Bank Scandal'. The financial institution at the centre of this scandal was the Bankgesellschaft Berlin (BGB), a public–private consortium of banks that included the Landesbank Berlin, the Berlin Hyp building society and a number of smaller banks. Founded in 1994, BGB reflected the ambition of the then-ruling Christian

Democratic Union (*Christlich-Demokratische Union Deutschlands*, CDU) to turn Berlin into a banking metropolis like London and Frankfurt. At the same time, however, the CDU's frontline politicians couldn't resist using BGB to enrich themselves as well. The main tool for this was various 'VIP funds': de-risked real estate funds tailor-made for political cronies.

The situation escalated when Klaus Landowsky – the boss of Berlin Hyp and, at the same time, deputy leader of the CDU parliamentary group – offered a loan of 600 million marks to a real estate company called Aubis, run by two old CDU colleagues. Hoping to profit from the legally enforced privatisation of East German housing stock,[29] Aubis bought up prefab concrete blocks in East Berlin, intending to renovate them and then relet the apartments at higher rents. All the risk was shifted from the investors to the public bank. When Aubis went bankrupt, it pulled down the whole Berlin banking system – and the city's budget.[30]

Klaus Wowereit, the new Social Democrat (*Sozialdemokratische Partei Deutschlands*, SPD) mayor, decided to tackle the crisis with a combination of harsh austerity and privatisation. This was when the large portfolios of housing in Berlin, both East and West, were sold off cheaply to private equity funds. This privatisation wasn't free of political profiteering either: as if by magic, several prominent SPD politicians involved in privatisation landed prominent jobs in the private equity sector after they resigned from office.[31] GSW and GEHAG were bought and sold several times by various private equity funds before eventually ending up with Deutsche Wohnen.

'What's picking a lock compared to buying shares?' As early as 1928, in *The Threepenny Opera*, the musical drama for which he is probably best known, the Berliner Bertolt Brecht warned about the ease with which corporations can 'steal' value that has been collectively produced. Corporations claim to contribute to the (market) value of the city, but all too often they turn our lively neighbourhoods into someone else's lifeless gold. As of January 2024, 91.8 per cent of Deutsche Wohnen's shareholders are other corporations or asset managers such as BlackRock. None of them is based in Berlin.[32]

Berlin has been made by Berliners. Even the market value of Berlin real estate stems primarily from its location: the cultural and economic attractiveness of the whole city, collectively created by its citizens, past and present. However, the market value is not the only value that matters. For Berliners, a functioning municipal housing system has been crucial to upholding other values too: freedom, equality and solidarity.

Berliners were not prepared to abandon these values. So when the corporate landlords first took over our housing, we rolled out our well-established repertoire of protest and resistance. We sang in the elevators and chanted on the streets. We occupied public squares, created networks and mobilised the union lawyers, who fought, case by case, for each person's right to stay. However, what worked with Herr Meier would not be enough to stop the corporations.

Hovering over Berlin, corporations were the Jabberwock (Figure 2.3) – a beast that can only be so large and powerful *because* it is fictional. Corporations are legal fictions, made by the law and living in the law. They can gradually leverage their legal power to *become* the law. Many academic books have been written about this.[33] T-INA Darling, a Berliner artist and DJ, wrote a song:

I bought your house
I bought your ground
For just about two million pounds
I'm gonna open your floor
Break through your door
I am the law
I am the law

Can real people ever win against a corporation – a monstrously empowered legal fiction? In Lewis Carroll's *Through the Looking-Glass*, to slay the Jabberwock a person needs to take the 'vorpal sword' in hand – a weapon that is equally powerful, because it is equally fictional.

7

In Prenzlauer Berg, where I live, there is a large block of streets that has only survived because some real people crafted a weapon from legal fictions. The quarter around Oderberger Strasse in East Berlin was home to punk rock and political

Figure 2.3 Jabberwock, a powerful fictional creature from Lewis Carroll's nonsense poem *Jabberwocky* featured in his book *Through the Looking-Glass, and What Alice Found There*. Illustrator: John Tenniel.
To kill this fictional creature, a person needs a fictional 'vorpal sword'.

dissidence. It didn't fit the image of the socialist regime, so in the 1980s the local government decided to demolish it.

Activists saved the block by applying the laws of an authoritarian state that had written them merely to serve as a cover. Leveraging formal rules of political participation, they managed, first of all, to take control of a local *Wohnbezirksausschuss* (a residential district committee, commonly referred to by the acronym WBA). WBAs were a subdivision of the National Front of the German Democratic Republic (GDR). The National Front was an alliance of political parties and organisations that secured the supremacy of the ruling Socialist Unity Party with a pretence of collaboration. It was just a façade to make socialism appear more democratic – yet it had formal legitimacy within the system.

'We analysed the laws of the GDR and found that the residential district committees could put up their own candidates [to the National Front],' one activist recalls. 'It was just that nobody had ever done that before.' The opposition effectively took over the local WBA. One of the activists was even elected to the Prenzlauer Berg district assembly, which made him the first opposition MP in the GDR, before the last parliamentary elections in March 1990.[34] The group had successfully prevented the demolition, and in the block of streets they had saved they created the 'Hirschhof', a neighbourhood meeting point with an open-air stage. The acronym WBA was transformed into *Wir Bleiben Alle*: We Are All Staying Put. After reunification, this became the main slogan for the housing struggle across the whole of Berlin (Figure 2.4). It often appears along with a symbol: a house raising the fist of its chimney to the sky.

But, in the end, not everyone did manage to stay put. Soon after the housing activists had saved their block, the people of the GDR overthrew the entire regime. East Berliners were ecstatic about their hard-won political freedom. Most had no idea at first that, as collateral for reunification, they were about to lose their homes.

Today, there are hardly any former East Germans living in Prenzlauer Berg. They couldn't afford to stay. First their buildings were 'reprivatised' – returned to the owners who had been

Figure 2.4 *Wir Bleiben Alle* – 'We Are All Staying Put': An occupied tenement block at Brunnenstrasse 183; occupiers evicted by the police on 27 October 2009
(*Source:* Jotquadrat/Wikipedia/Creative Commons)

expropriated after the Second World War by the East German state. But because the buildings required extensive renovation, only 5 to 8 per cent of the original owners wanted, or could afford, to keep them.[35] Hardly any East Berliners could afford to buy these buildings – the income and wealth gap between East and West was considerable. For the richest West Germans, however, the buildings were cheap. With some specially legislated tax exemptions, they were virtually free: the majority of the purchase and renovation costs became tax deductible.

These tax deductions only made sense for affluent people – and so Prenzlauer Berg was effectively donated to the West German upper classes. In 1997, *Der Spiegel* described it as 'the greatest tax present of all time', and Saxony's conservative finance minister Georg Milbradt spoke of it as 'capital formation for the West'.[36] East Berliners tried to keep their homes by occupying the buildings. The fact that they couldn't became a long-standing source of anger and frustration at the new system, which in this respect had not delivered on the constitutional promise of freedom.[37]

I too live in a house from which East Germans are long gone. I learned the history of Prenzlauer Berg from A. and M., two scholar-activists from East Berlin who became my dear friends. M. lives in a housing cooperative, and has managed to stay in Prenzlauer Berg. A. has moved out. Whenever I walked around the district with M., he would tell me the history of every house. But neither M. nor A. have ever blamed me for being a 'gentrifier'. They believe in fixing the broken system, not putting the blame on those who come here searching for home. For Berlin to feel like home, we must keep on making it home together: East and West, migrants and Germans, those who were born here and you who have just arrived. *Wir bleiben alle*: We are all free to stay.

On the night of A.'s forty-seventh birthday, I stayed home. I fell asleep breastfeeding my eight-week-old daughter, which was how I missed the party that, according to urban legend, was the birthplace of Deutsche Wohnen & Co. enteignen. Of course, it couldn't just have been this one party; revolutions start in many places at once, as if spreading through the air. Still, in certain moments and places the air condenses, and potential is transformed into energy. This is what must have happened that night at Aquarium, a venue right next to the Kotti. It was October 2017.

Let me tell you what I heard. The Aquarium was packed – it must have been. A. is Berlin's ultimate scholar-activist: diligent and legendary, brilliant and humble. Electro music blasted from the speakers, mixed with 1980s punk rock. The playlist will definitely have included 'Transmission' by Joy Division, one of A.'s all-time favourites. There's a line in the song: *The things that we've learnt are no longer enough*. I doubt that anyone there was thinking about the lyrics, but there were enough people who were feeling precisely this: *The things that we've learnt are no longer enough*.

That night, T-INA Darling was the DJ. But the dancing didn't start until 2 a.m., because the room where it all happened was supposed to be the dancefloor. M. was a bit irritated; he was eager to dance. He too had a small child at home, *and this could be a party, for once, not another work meeting*. But there were so many people in the room! Apparently R. had spent a whole vacation trying to figure out how this could work, talking it through with a bunch of friends on some Greek island. This, here, could be the perfect sounding board – a group of people who knew Berlin inside out.

We will never know who was the first to come up with the idea – and it doesn't matter. By then, we all knew we had to tackle the problem at its roots. We would not be able to change the logic of finance, so we needed to shield our homes from this logic. We didn't need to 'smash the system', only to save our system from being smashed by the inhumane power of the corporate Jabberwock.

If the solution was hiding, it was hiding in plain sight. Right at the heart of the *Grundgesetz* there lay a 'vorpal sword': Article 15. It was a legal fiction of the highest order: a fundamental right forged by Germany's constituent power. This all-but-forgotten right allows for land, natural resources and means of production to be made public property for the purpose of 'socialisation' (*Vergesellschaftung*). As a democratic weapon, Article 15 comes with one proviso: the socialised property must be held collectively by the people. It cannot simply be subordinated to the state. It must be democratically managed.

The mighty sword of Article 15 has always been there, just like the constitution. Suddenly, everyone wondered why we had never dared to use it. Article 15 offered a *practical* revolution: lawful, affordable, good.

That night, the question was not *if* – the question was *how*. That's why the dancing didn't start until 2 a.m. And after that, people didn't want to wait any longer. The DJ put on 'Waiting Room', a 1989 post-hardcore song by Fugazi, one of A.'s all-time favourites:

I'm planning a big surprise
I'm gonna fight for what I wanna be
And I won't make the same mistakes
Because I know how much time that wastes and function
Function is the key!

And then they danced and danced, as if our freedom depended on it, pounding the ground to summon the Berliner spirit. And I danced with them too, until I woke up: free to be home, embracing the future.

Figure 3.1 The spectres of expropriation in front of the Deutsche Wohnen
Headquarters in Frankfurt, 18 June 2019
(*Source:* DWE Archive)

What you're showing here is the ugly Berlin, the loud Berlin. This is the unserious Berlin. This is Berlin that, in my opinion, has no future. Michael Zahn, CEO of Deutsche Wohnen, in a panel discussion with a DWE activist

Expropriate!
Albert Einstein, Berliner, a vocal supporter of the 1926 referendum on the expropriation of princes (*Fürstenenteignung*)

BERLIN BECOMES HIGH-RISK CAPITAL

The Law and the Movement

1

Two careful lines drawn diagonally in an X across the circle. First one line, then the second; and, if I didn't stop her, a little heart as well.

'Mama, how do we say ballot paper in Polish?'

'Karta do głosowania. You know, darling, the cross is a bit like a heart already – it's a way of telling the government how we feel about it.'

It's 26 September 2021 – Election Day. In addition to choosing the new national and municipal governments, Berliners are voting in the referendum on expropriating corporate landlords and socialising their housing stock by implementing Article 15. The referendum has been organised by a grassroots campaign, 'Deutsche Wohnen & Co. enteignen'. I joined DWE in 2019.

My daughter marks *Ja* and passes me the ballot. I wonder whether her help is illegal. The clerk at the entrance initially told me I couldn't take Mira with me into the voting cabin. It's to preserve the secrecy of the ballot, she says. My daughter might influence my vote.

As an activist, I regret not thinking of this earlier! The pre-schooler lobby could easily have swung the vote for us by throwing tantrums on Election Day. All they want is their own bedrooms! (Figure 3.2)

'But she's 4!' I take my chances with the election supervisors.

'Can she read?'

'Not yet.'

'OK. She can go in with you.'

Figure 3.2 Mira on Election Day
(*Source:* Joanna Kusiak)

My little lobbyist can, of course, draw.

Twelve hours later, crowded into a vast hall at the BUFA film studios in Berlin-Tempelhof for election evening, we're watching K. on a big screen. He is talking, live, to the spokesperson of an association explicitly created to lobby against us. *Neue Wege für Berlin* claims to be a social movement, but it consists mainly of real estate professionals. In 2019, journalists revealed that this 'social movement' had asked its members to pay a membership contribution of €2,750 each.[1]

A big chunk of this money has presumably been spent on petitioning against DWE. After DWE collected 77,001 signatures for the first phase of preparing for the referendum, *Neue Wege für Berlin* hired a professional agency to collect signatures 'for affordable housing'. Only the fine print on the signature collection sheet specified that this affordable housing would be achieved by abolishing the *Mietendeckel* – a five-year cap on rents legislated by the government in 2020 – and preventing socialisation.[2] Even so, the paid agency workers collected only a fraction of the signatures collected in support of socialisation by unpaid DWE volunteers.

'The campaign has put a finger on something that's a sore point for the city,' the lobbyist is saying. He quickly adds that, according to his association's experts, what DWE proposes is not legally viable. The journalist cuts him off, reminding him that there are plenty of legal analysts who assert otherwise. However, the journalist adds, the leading mayoral candidate, Franziska Giffey from the Social Democrats, sees socialisation as a 'red line' she never wants to cross, while Bettina Jarasch from the Green Party says socialisation would be *ultima ratio*, a last resort.

'We will soon know where Berliners stand,' says K.

Almost 11 p.m., and still no results. After vanishing from the big screen, K. reappears among us in the hall, and we gather round him, excited. Did he hear anything at the television studios? Any leaks? Any predictions?

No. No leaks, and no official predictions. But once the cameras were off, the real estate association's spokesperson approached K. and shook his hand.

'I'm a realist,' the lobbyist said. 'You will win.'

2

We won. Of course we won! With more than 1 million 'Yes' votes, Deutsche Wohnen & co. enteignen got more support than any of the political parties participating in the general election. Still, if a real estate lobbyist was able to predict our victory from the standpoint of political realism, this pointed to a critical transition. Back in 2017, when DWE's strategy was first discussed at A.'s birthday party, even some of the activists were sceptical that the idea of expropriation could actually win a majority. The referendum victory was a side-effect of an even more remarkable feat by DWE: creating a major shift in what was considered politically 'realistic' (Figure 3.3). How had we managed to make the impossible realistic?

At first, the prospect of expropriation looked like a big, bold nothing. Anything that has never been done before starts with a confrontation with the void. This negative aspect – the impossibility of creation, the shadow of failure – is always present. It's here, too: if you peer behind the letters of this book, you'll see the blank page I once had to stare at. But if you persist in confronting nothingness with your being, *something* will inevitably emerge. At first, it might be something phantasmal: an almost-nothing, a spectre.

The spectres of expropriation materialised in the daytime. These were real, human ghosts, down-to-earth and dressed for the job, in white bedsheets with cut-out holes for their eyes.

Figure 3.3 Election evening games: Will it be possible to overthrow the rule of corporate landlords?
(*Source:* Ian Clotworthy/DWE)

They were nothing like Karl Marx's spectres of communism that were once said to be haunting Europe.[3] They were not ideological, and they were not a metaphor. They were angry. In June 2018, a small group of them appeared outside Deutsche Wohnen's Berlin office, holding banners and chanting 'Expropriate!' *Enteignen, enteignen!* Very few people saw them; there were only a couple of journalists to take pictures. But the ghosts saw one another, and they believed in themselves – as spectres.

The spectres of expropriation preceded DWE as a movement. They recruited themselves from the Berlin-wide network of Deutsche Wohnen tenants. In 2016, in response to a wave of rent increases by Deutsche Wohnen, some activists launched a working group they called 'Jumpstart' (*AG Starthilfe*). The group's mission was to help tenants to organise, so that people on an estate could come together and challenge individual rent increases collectively.

'Jumpstart' activists devised a procedure called an 'Organising Blitz'. They would identify the most proactive tenants, meet them at their housing estate, and offer them a short training course on the principles of organisation. Then trainers and trainees would disperse for a couple of hours to knock on people's doors, tell them about possible ways of dealing with the rent increases and invite them to a community meeting two weeks later. The response was huge, and tenants started to connect across estates, as well.

If you talked to the spectres of expropriation – those few bold tenants who, dressed in old bedsheets, stood outside a multi-billion-euro corporation and declared that they would expropri-ate it – they would tell you that, in a democracy, you always have more power than you think. You only need to be aware of the power you already have.

The seeds for DWE's referendum victory were planted long before the launch of the campaign. Berliners have been training themselves in public referenda since 2011, when the city voted to de-privatise (buy back) the Berlin water company. The 2014 Tempelhofer Feld referendum was another great success, preventing luxury real-estate development on a former airport and maintaining it as an iconically non-designed Berlin public space.

The 'rent referendum' (*Mietenvolksentscheid*), coinitiated in 2015 by a grassroots movement called Kotti & Co., was never held. Its initiators made some formal mistakes in their proposed legislation, and so were unable to proceed with the referendum, even though they had a lot of public support. This early failure may have been crucial for DWE's future success: the activists learned that, in order to operate politically on a legal footing, one has to adapt to the very precise terms of the law.

By the time the spectres of expropriation appeared outside Deutsche Wohnen, another activists' working group (*Vergesellschaftungs-AG*) had already sketched out the legal strategy for expropriating corporate landlords. But no journalists were there to take pictures of that.

Of the small number of activists who first conceptualised the strategy for socialisation, none was a trained lawyer. Back in 2017, most lawyers barely remembered that Article 15 even existed. Some later claimed it was an 'empty clause' that had become 'obsolete' from lack of use.[4] But if you are not a lawyer, you apply common sense. Can it be that a constitutional right expires, or goes off, like an old piece of cheese, forgotten at the back of the fridge? This didn't seem reasonable. Once the activists had drafted the first strategic documents, they consulted a few friendly lawyers. And boy were the lawyers surprised! *Actually, this could work!* The boundaries of the realistic were slowly giving way, starting with the legal profession.

But there is no beaten track to implementing Article 15 – and the law is a jungle of technicalities. Learning from the mistakes of the 2015 'rent referendum', the activists trod carefully. Berlin's state constitution allows for two different types of referendum: a legislative referendum (*Gesetzesvolksentscheid*) and a resolution referendum (*Beschlussvolksentscheid*). The first puts a complete piece of legislation to the vote. The second garners political support for a project, which the Senate then legislates itself. Because Article 15 was new terrain, even for experienced lawyers, DWE went for the second option: a resolution referendum.

A resolution referendum allowed DWE not to rush into drafting the appropriate legislation, risking a formal mistake. But the activists didn't rush the referendum, either. They took a whole year to

gather the relevant legal expertise, during which time the movement was already using Article 15 as leverage in the public debate.
Because while expropriating 240,000 apartments may sound 'radical' and 'impossible', it is much harder to dismiss a fundamental
right inscribed in the *Grundgesetz* as a radical fantasy.

'I wouldn't have thought this possible.' Frank Plasberg paused
in the middle of his prime-time television show *Hart aber Fair*
('Hard but Fair') to reflect on what was happening. 'For the last
eleven minutes, we've been talking seriously about expropriating a corporation in Germany.'[5] It was March 2019. A few weeks
earlier, *Tagesspiegel* had published a poll showing that almost
55 per cent of Berliners considered the expropriation of corporate landlords to be a 'reasonable' option.[6]

On 6 April 2019, amid the crowd of 40,000 people who had
joined the 'Rent Insanity' (*Mietenwahnsinn*) demonstration in
Berlin, DWE started to collect the 20,000 signatures required
for the first stage of the referendum. By the end of that first day,
the activists had already collected more than half of the signatures they needed.

Two months later, the spectres of expropriation showed up to
spook shareholders at Deutsche Wohnen's general assembly in
Frankfurt. This was just a few days after the campaign submit-
ted its petition with 77,001 signatures – almost four times more
than the requirement.

Soon afterwards, the government legislated the *Mietendeckel*, a
five-year cap on rents. Alarmed by the success of the petition, the
governing SPD party pitched the *Mietendeckel* as a 'milder' alternative to socialisation. When I interviewed a lawyer who co-
wrote the *Mietendeckel* legislation, she said she saw the rental
freeze as a side-effect of socialisation suddenly being seen as an
option available within the system. What was previously considered 'too radical' became a 'mild alternative'.[7]

'Dear shareholders, we are your biggest investment risk!' This
was how S., surrounded by the bedsheet-wearing spectres of
expropriation, opened the DWE press conference outside
Deutsche Wohnen's headquarters in Frankfurt. The day the
government announced it would freeze rents for five years,
Deutsche Wohnen stocks fell by 8.7 per cent. S. advised

shareholders to sell their shares immediately. Democracy – popular, and constitutional – was turning Berlin into high-risk capital.

The frontiers of political realism were now shifting too quickly for some. Andreas Geisel, Berlin's senator for interior, decided to slow it down. His office was responsible for checking the legal viability of this initial referendum proposal. Once this was confirmed, the campaign could move on to the second stage – which meant collecting more signatures. However, there was no official deadline by which the Berlin Senate had to reply. It had in fact already commissioned a legal opinion, which had confirmed a few months earlier that the proposal was indeed valid,[8] but Herr Geisel's office did not respond for more than eleven months.

In September 2020, the movement filed an urgent appeal (*Eilantrag*) against the Senate for its inaction, after which the Senate completed the check in two days. The movement then asked to review the Senate's documents using the Freedom of Information Act. Together with some journalists, DWE was able to reveal that the Senate's delay was intentional. On the day of the DWE lawsuit, one of Herr Geisel's coworkers wrote in an internal email: 'If the lawsuit is accepted, we won't stand a chance.'[9]

The campaign turned the Senate's delaying tactics into an advantage, using the extra time for internal restructuring. The second stage of the referendum campaign would require activists to collect 175,000 valid, physical signatures in just four months. But now everyone was staying home. The global COVID-19 pandemic had started.

Unlike many other social initiatives, DWE grew exponentially throughout the pandemic. On the one hand, people *felt*, acutely, how vital it was to have a home – and were even more afraid of rent increases in the light of COVID-related recession. On the other hand, in times of general uncertainty, DWE's legal-political framework provided people with a clear and measurable goal. The activists surfed the wave of online socialising to grow a network of *Kiezteams*, DWE's neighbourhood units. Once the strict terms of the first lockdown were relaxed, their members were able to meet physically in the local parks, provided they maintained social distance. Amid the global loneliness of the pandemic, DWE effectively organised people to meet their neighbours even *more*.

Almost 350,000 signatures – more than twice as many as were needed to organise the referendum – were collected between February and June 2021, amid intermittent lockdowns, without mass events, and with lousy weather persisting until mid-May. The *Kiezteams* competed internally to get record numbers of signatures, while also supporting one another, sending activists from the central districts to help also in the neighbourhoods on the periphery (Figure 3.4). Then, in the run-up to the referendum, the *Kiezteams* campaigned door-to-door. Door-to-door campaigning is very unusual in German culture. But the ground for this had been prepared when the 'Jumpstart' group was teaching tenants how to organise themselves, back when expropriation still looked like a big, bold nothing. Or like a spectre: down-to-earth, and dressed for work.

Figure 3.4 Collecting signatures in Berlin-Marzahn
(*Source:* Ian Clotworthy/DWE)

3

When I tell my daughter ghost stories at bedtime, she sometimes asks me if the story is *real*. With some stories, I'm not sure how to answer. When a group of people dressed up as ghosts appear in public with a copy of the *Grundgesetz*, are they *real* spectres of expropriation? You can see their shoes poking out from underneath the bedsheets. And yet their appearance caused stocks to fall. Trick or treat?

The referendum organised by DWE was certainly real. My daughter remembers putting a real ballot paper into a real box. Real people counted the votes of other real people, and it was the most successful referendum in Berlin's history.[10] Still, its results were never implemented. Is democracy real, or is it just a story I tell my daughter at bedtime? 'Some stories are just fictions,' I explain to Mira, 'but there are some fictions that we have to make real together.'

On 26 September 2023, exactly two years after we celebrated the results of the first referendum, Deutsche Wohnen & Co. enteignen announced that it would organise a second one (Figure 3.5). This time, it will be a legislative referendum (*Gesetzesvolksentscheid*). The movement has commissioned a renowned law firm specialising in public and constitutional law to write the legislation. The lawyers' fees and other campaign expenses have been crowdfunded. The campaign's new slogan is 'Our Berlin – Our Home – Our Law'.

Another slogan of the new referendum is: *Allet mussma selba machn* (Figure 3.6). In the Berliner dialect, this means: 'We have to do everything ourselves.' We have to write the socialisation law ourselves, even though one million Berliners had already ordered the government to do so, using the resolution referendum as prescribed by the Constitution of Berlin. But a resolution referendum is a *political* tool: it is not legally binding.

To implement the results of the resolution referendum, the government would have to write appropriate legislation. Both the mayors who have governed since the referendum – first Franziska Giffey of the Social Democrats (SPD), then Kai

Figure 3.5 DWE announces the second referendum in front of the Rotes Rathaus (Berlin City Hall), 23 September 2023
(*Source:* Ian Clotworthy/DWE)

Wegner of the Christian Democrats (CDU) – have opposed social-isation. Their resistance is hardly surprising: both their parties have been receiving campaign funding from the real estate lobby. The only way to bypass the government's inaction is to write the law ourselves and put it to a direct vote.

Was DWE politically naïve in trusting that politicians would implement the will of the majority? Shouldn't the initiative have gone straight for a legislation referendum, in the first round? Maybe – but I don't think so. Because back in 2017, when DWE first launched its campaign, Article 15 was like an unloaded gun, and everyone had forgotten what the bullet looked like.

The power of Article 15 is both real and fictional. It's the power of a legal fiction. To call something a 'fiction' might sound dismissive, but the normative power of the law depends on legal fictions.[11] The law creates fictions by abstracting from

Figure 3.6 'We have to do everything ourselves': The spectres of expropriation dancing in front of the Rotes Rathaus (*Source:* Ian Clotworthy/DWE)

reality, then empowers these fictions to transform reality. That a corporation can count as a person is a legal fiction with real-life consequences. But rights are legal fictions as well. As suggested by Eric Voegelin, the idea of constitutionally guaranteed rights may be nothing more than a superstitious belief in the power of law.[12] For what does a constitutional right to socialisation mean if nothing has been socialised?

The rule of law's cardinal fiction – one that sustains its democratic legitimacy – is the idea of a free and equal subject. Born into a social context, we are not born equal: in our wealth, or in our capacities. Depending on the circumstances of our lives, we do not enjoy the same amount of freedom. By denying these structural inequalities, the law can perpetuate them. But by insisting on freedom and equality, the law can also pull reality closer to fiction: it can make us *count* as equals, thereby making the system balance out some of the existing inequalities. That the law considers us 'free and equal' is not, therefore, a neutral thing: it contains both a brutal lie and the utopian horizon of democracy.

The power of a legal fiction is a power potential: in order to shape reality, legal fictions must be empowered. What empowers a legal fiction? First, the law itself. Law is a self-reproducing ('autopoietic') system that constantly replicates its own elements and structures.[13] Each legal textbook and each judicial ruling strengthens some legal arguments while omitting others, creating precedents and tendencies in jurisprudence.

Legal fictions are also empowered by legal experts. Because what legal theorists claim – that the law is a self-reproducing system – is itself a legal fiction, an abstracted truth. The law reproduces 'itself' in the hands of the lawyers. Lawyers are not neutral cogs in the machine of legal reproduction: they actively shape it. The law consists of language, and it is therefore malleable and subject to interpretation. To interpret the law is to decide its meaning, and the impact it would have on reality. The leeway of interpretation is the inner politics of the law.

Private attorneys are lawyers whose job is to infuse the law with politics that are beneficial to their clients. The wealthiest clients – which nowadays are usually corporations – hire more and better lawyers. That's why, when it comes to securing and multiplying wealth, the law has never been the static rules of the game: 'The rules themselves have become the centre of the game.'[14] The fraudulent legal engineering revealed by the Panama Papers is only the logical consequence of private lawyers' efforts to serve their high-paying clients.

Another strain of politics is brought to the law by conviction-driven activist lawyers, either self-appointed or supported by popular mobilisation. In the midst of all this are public lawyers: judges and legal officials appointed by the system. They too are people, and as such they are never entirely free of their own agendas. But they are appointed by the system to maintain the law – to hold within the legal system a protected space for reasoning about what is right and fair, and to 'morph politics and produce a universalising argument'.[15]

There is a formal gate through which politics enters the law officially and unapologetically: legislation. Written in legal terms but empowered by politics, legislation is where the contingency of politics stabilises into a 'system'. In a representative democracy, it's usually the job of parliament to legislate, and the job of the legal system – via the constitutional court, for example – to ensure that the legislation does not violate the terms of the law. To transform the system via new legislation, you need support from both politics and the law.

When DWE was starting out as a movement, it had hardly any support on either side – a small group of activists with a supposedly 'obsolete' legal clause. The ingenuity of the DWE strategy lay in trusting Article 15 more than the lawyers did, and using it as leverage to support the political postulate of expropriation with the normative power of the *Grundgesetz*. The power of the *Grundgesetz* has mobilised the people, and the power of the people has mobilised the lawyers. In this way, legal expertise was effectively 'outsourced' by the movement: as soon as the first polls showed that the majority supported socialisation, the Berlin Senate, political parties and think tanks started commissioning legal opinions, the overwhelming majority of which confirmed the legal viability of socialisation.

As of 2023, this has been also confirmed by the final report of the Expert Commission on Socialisation. The commission, consisting mainly of constitutional lawyers with a few experts on housing finance, spent a whole year deliberating the legal nuts and bolts of the DWE project. Mayor Franziska Giffey, who set up the commission, made almost no effort to conceal the fact that its real political aim was to delay or even avoid implementing socialisation. Yet the commission's final report ultimately provided a solid legal basis for a second referendum, having mobilised legal expertise to clear a range of issues crucial for the legislation project.

A political battle is being fought within the law regarding which legal fictions will be empowered and which will remain dormant. The most anti-democratic way of dealing with the law is to conceal this battle, or pretend that its terms are always the neutral domain of independent experts.

Rights are legal fictions that need to be empowered. There are no wealthy clients willing to hire the best lawyers to protect

popular rights, so the people must participate in the law, mobil-
ising legal expertise not through money, but by popular
summons. Because it's not only lawyers who can empower the
legal fictions of rights; it's also the people. That's why, in a
democracy, the law is far too important to be left to lawyers.

4

I never wanted to study law and, formally, I never did. Where
I come from, poor kids studied law to stop being poor, and rich
kids studied law because that was what their parents did.
I wanted to understand the world, so I studied philosophy and
social sciences. I also never planned to become a 'scholar-activist': it's a label that was given to me only after I left Poland.
In Warsaw, most of my university professors had been involved
with the Solidarność movement; engaging with reality was considered a crucial aspect of intellectual education. From a close
family member, who runs a public philosophy seminar in a
small town attended by artists and shopkeepers alike, I learned
that thinking can also be a form of public service.

In Berlin, I chose to turn thinking into a living. I became an
academic. But once I settled into my Berlin freedom, the brutal-
ity of the Polish shock therapy struck me with renewed force.
I returned to Warsaw as a researcher, determined to make sense
of the many urban crises triggered by privatisation and deregulation, a state-driven dismantling of the state. People called these
overlapping crises 'chaos', because it felt as if a blind force had
taken control of our city. But the more data I collected, the
clearer it became that this chaos was *organised* into multiple
orders of profit-driven dispossession.[16] I teamed up with
Warsaw's social movements to analyse what later became
known as 'Reprivatisationgate', Poland's most spectacular case
of legal corruption.

In the early 2010s, Warsaw was losing ground – literally, and
for real. Thousands of tenants were being evicted, as their buildings were allegedly being 'restituted' to the historical owners
dispossessed by the communist regime, and a budgetary crisis

was looming because of the scale of the compensation claims. But the odd thing was this: the parliament never legislated property restitution because of Warsaw's complicated history. After the city was razed to the ground by the Nazis, the people rebuilt it in a collective effort, on a different urban grid, with public funding.[17] What was nationalised in 1945 was a pile of rubble. What was now to be 'returned' was critical public infrastructure: schools, university buildings, public parks and housing. The issue was simply too contentious. More than twenty proposed restitution bills were rejected, one after the other, by consecutive parliaments of various political colours.

There was no restitution law, no democratic mandate for the restitution – and yet newspapers were reporting restitution-driven evictions on an almost daily basis. How was this possible? The answer, I discovered, was the legal fictions. It turned out that the judiciary had engineered a discreet path to proceed with restitution on a case-by-case basis, ignoring the political conflict and bypassing the democratic process.

Combining incompatible legal acts from Poland's three different political systems (pre-war democracy, state socialism and the current one), the lawyers bent the letter of the law and broke its spirit. They did things such as use a post-war reconstruction decree from 1945 as a tool for privatisation, or designate a twenty-family tenement block as a 'single-family house' in order to privatise it.[18] The talk was of 'historical justice', but most of the land was being 'restituted' to professional businessmen who had bought restitution claims – cheaply, because with no restitution legislation in place, the claims were deemed worthless. In this way, a small clique of businessmen – many of whom were lawyers – took over Warsaw's prime real estate.[19]

By the time the legal corruption behind Reprivatisationgate was finally exposed – by activists, journalists and scholars working hand in hand to crack open the legal black box – it was too late. Warsaw's stolen land had been laundered, just as the law is able to launder drug money: by passing it through a chain of legitimate transactions. Warsaw's best apartments, rebuilt by the people under state socialism, then stolen *through* the law under – or rather, despite – democracy, had become 'clean' investment properties.

In 2016, sitting in one such investment apartment in Warsaw, I drafted the proposal for a research project that underlies the book you are now reading. The apartment had been rented for me through a well-known online portal, by an institution that had invited me to speak at a conference about – ironically – the Polish housing crisis. I immediately recognised the building from my research. It was very clean and expensive: all the apartments had been converted into offices and temporary rentals.

Architecturally, this Warsaw short-term rental was much like my Berlin home: an early twentieth-century tenement with spacious rooms and high ceilings. And in each case the current status of both these apartments was the result of the way legal fictions had played out politically within judicial proceedings. The Warsaw tenants had been evicted through legal fictions. I, through legal fictions, was able to stay in Berlin.

So here was my project: to explore and democratise the discreet politics of legal fictions. Crafting legal fictions is a standard legal procedure. But the more the technical jargon of the law conceals these operations, the easier it becomes to smuggle power agendas into the law. Once this mechanism was exposed, the inner politics of the law could be democratised without forfeiting the law's systemic independence. The lawyers would still make decisions about the terms of the legal system – but while the lawyers work the letter of the law, the people can protect its spirit.

I planned to work closely with the Berlin tenants' unions, learning how lawyers like Frau Tams make strategic use of legal technicalities in defending tenants. In January 2017, I pitched this project to King's College, Cambridge, which agreed to fund it. In May 2018 – halfway through my maternity leave – I gave a talk about my project at the Humboldt University of Berlin. I argued that we had to reclaim the law as a democratic tool for social change. A student approached me afterwards, asking if I had heard of the campaign that had just been launched: Deutsche Wohnen & Co. enteignen.

When I first met with some of DWE's activists, I realised that everything I wanted to research they were about to explore in practice. And so I joined the movement, and I cannot neatly separate whether I joined because of my research objectives or because of my convictions. But having studied the biographies of the Solidarność intellectuals – reading books, participating in the home seminars they organised for their students and also researching their corruption, as I did in my first job – I have learned one thing in particular: it was not in the 1980s, when they were out on the streets fighting for the ethics of solidarity, but in the 1990s that some of them – by then in secure academic posts and playing the role of the neutral expert – stopped acknowledging their bias.

5

The Berliner Kurt Lewin, a social psychologist who first conceived the term 'action research', was also the first to use the term 'feedback' in a social science context, borrowing it from electrical engineering. He visualised action research as a spiral of steps: each step is an independent cycle of gathering information through research, strategising an overall plan, strategising the next step, intervening in the system and evaluating the results of the intervention. The learning acquired through each cycle is implemented in the planning phase of the next cycle.

The purpose of action-research is strategic, which means there is a strong incentive to avoid partiality and wishful thinking. Any too-neat research conclusion will quickly be destroyed in practice. Academics often joke about 'Reviewer 2', a humorous designation for the anonymous, spiteful colleague who finds, or even invents, faults in your research paper, no matter how hard you've tried. For an action researcher, the real 'Reviewer 2' is practice.

But being a scholar-activist is a delicate task for reasons other than methodology. You need to learn to navigate the tension between being a member of the movement while also being an external observer. As a scholar, the purpose behind my methodological rigour is to speak with authority about my research findings. The movement, however, strives for democracy: DWE avoids giving one voice greater authority than others. Just like the law, democracy is driven by a normative fiction of freedom and equality. And so, as we take on different roles within the movement – some more visible than others – we still take care that we all *count* as equal in the movement's decision-making process.

The principle of equality in decision-making translates into DWE's approaches to expertise. On the one hand, democracy does not mean rejecting the expertise; especially when working with the law, we rely a lot on lawyers' precise, technical advice. On the other hand, no expertise – not even legal – is allowed to dominate the discussion unquestioned. In situations where the movement made the decision to rely on external experts – for example, when hiring a law firm to draw up the legislation for the second referendum – the movement also delegates a small group of activists to mediate between the firm and the movement, translating and explaining the experts' decisions during the plena so they can be followed or questioned by the movement's democratic grassroots.

The methodological value of being an action-researcher is not limited to any specific kind of expertise. Rather, the value of the method lies in constantly switching between the 'immersive' position of an activist and a detached scholarly perspective. This makes it possible analytically to grasp patterns that occur within the movement, while also developing a feel for the way these patterns are forged on an everyday level.

There is only one consensus within DWE: to socialise housing using Article 15. We disagree about many other things, often fiercely. Nor is it the case that the things we disagree about are politically insignificant. But the one thing we all agree on – the socialisation of housing using Article 15 – is important enough that disagreement becomes constructive. That's why, viewed from the outside, DWE strategy is based on paradoxes. A paradox is simply 'a better witness to truth'.[20]

First of all: DWE is radical – but it's also radically legal. In referring to the *Grundgesetz*, it mobilises the state's constituent power (*verfassungsgebende Gewalt*) to curb misuses of this power, transforming the system from the inside. Not unlike *Solidarność* in the 1980s, it gains legitimacy by holding the system to its promises by both political *and* legal means. As a radically legal movement, DWE mobilises the power of the people and the power of the system simultaneously.

That is why – secondly – DWE is simultaneously anti-systemic and pro-systemic. This is reflected in the campaign's use of two terms: 'expropriation' (*Enteignung*), its main political slogan, and 'socialisation' (*Vergesellschaftung*), which is the proper legal term for what DWE is proposing. By postulating to 'expropriate' corporate landlords, DWE taps into people's anger at the dysfunctionality of the system. But it mobilises this anger to renew the system rather than destroy it. Proposing a radical change, DWE also plans to embed this change within the existing legal framework.

Thirdly, DWE is a single-cause movement that builds a broad social base by approaching this cause from multiple angles. The vision of socialisation is holistic, addressing the needs of different people and sectors. DWE thinks through the impact of socialisation on the local economy, the social welfare system and ecological transformation. Within its own structures, DWE commits to inclusion without striving for consensus on identity politics. It thus avoids sectarian splits while maintaining a strong focus.

Fourthly, DWE maintains productive tension between the concrete and the universal. It builds a community, starting from the concrete experience of living in a particular neighbourhood, then empowers this community using systemic abstractions. It connects all the dimensions of globalisation: it is a local movement that uses the national legal framework to counter global finance. This approach, simultaneously functional and territorial, is reflected in the way DWE is internally organised into task-oriented working groups (*Arbeitsgruppen*, AGs) and local neighbourhood units (*Kiezteams*).

Fifthly, DWE does not believe in the day after the revolution. Democracy – the normative ideal that all people meaningfully participate in governing themselves – is a utopia that must be approximated, but it will never be completed. In order to move ahead, DWE mediates between its vision and the status quo, working to close the gap between them. It also works towards widening this gap at its other end, pushing the boundaries of what is perceived as 'achievable' within the current system. Because democracy is not just a destination to move towards. Democracy is also the movement.

6

By the time DWE organises its second referendum, my daughter – born in the same year as the movement – will be nearly 10. For DWE, it will have been a decade of organising: persistently, voluntarily, unpaid. At peak moments in the referendum campaign, the movement mobilised more than 3,000 people, and there is a relatively stable core of more than 100 activists. But if a popular movement is successful, diverse and growing, internal conflicts are inevitable. There is also push-back from without; the boundaries of political realism are not easily moved. How has DWE maintained its energy and efficiency, in spite of internal and external resistance?

To stay alive, a movement needs two things: energy and structure. The structure derives from analysis: it aims to break strategy down into tasks, direct energy towards these tasks and evaluate results in order to update the strategy. The energy comes from emotions. No matter how rational the strategy is, people must *feel like moving*, especially when all movement seems blocked.

Most social movements are born of anger. Anger is a crucial political emotion, as it is 'loaded with information and energy'.[21] Its healthy root is care, including self-care. We get angry because our needs are not met, or because someone destroys something that we value. Berlin's tenants were angry because they feared losing their freedom – either by losing their home, or by spending a disproportionate amount of their salary on rent.

DWE provided a structure that channelled people's anger into a legal form: the right to socialisation as inscribed in Article 15. Because this form was partially empty, DWE used the energy of anger to build a campaign that fills Article 15 with meaning. In this way, DWE mobilised people's righteous anger to reclaim a constitutional right. Because anger doesn't need to break the law – it can also renew it.

Somewhere in this process, anger transforms into joy. A. tells me she learned this from Brazil's Landless Workers' Movement: 'You join because of what you want to change, but you stay because of how you feel.' Because of the way A.'s laughter ripples through what is technically a research interview, I can *feel* that she means it.

Born in Brazil, A. joined DWE through the 'Jumpstart' working group. She then realised that many of the tenants do not speak German and, as migrants, would have no right to vote in the DWE referendum. For them, A. launched 'Right to the City', an English-speaking working group within DWE. She also brought *mística* to DWE: a procedure that is indeed somewhat mystical, which has become an essential element of DWE's alchemy of emotions.[22]

What fruit would you be, if you were a fruit? As a lemon, I, too, take pleasure in producing raw facial expressions. That's why I can't help but laugh when A. tells me about the time she first proposed to some 'serious' German activists working on the law that each work meeting could start with a question like that, or perhaps a reading from a poem, or singing a song. It allows people to connect to their feelings, and to one another, before moving on to a 'technical' working agenda. Before you are an activist, you are a person with a soul.

Starting with the Right to the City working group, a sense of audacious playfulness has gradually disseminated throughout the movement. Nearly all of DWE's 'serious' public events and political hearings are now accompanied by something light and joyful, like performances by the official DWE cheerleading squad, or an 'expropriation fashion show': haute couture in yellow and purple. 'At first, everyone was asking, "What does it all have to do with expropriation?" I say, "Nothing and every-thing,"' laughs A., 'because there will be no expropriation with-out a strong community.'

DWE's dual organising principle – that of community-building, and that of legal and procedural push – was already present in the merger of the legal-oriented 'socialisation' working group with the neighbourhood-activating 'Jumpstart'. The development of the movement's organisational structure (Figure 3.7) further reflects this logic. Parallel to the working groups, there are fourteen 'Kiezteams', neighbourhood units focused on the local community. When making decisions, DWE relies on a mixture of direct and representative democracy. Working groups and Kiezteams send their representatives to the 'Coordination Circle' (Ko-Kreis), a managing team that gathers input from the movement's structures and drafts strategy proposals. These proposals are discussed and voted on at the bi-weekly general assembly (Plenum).

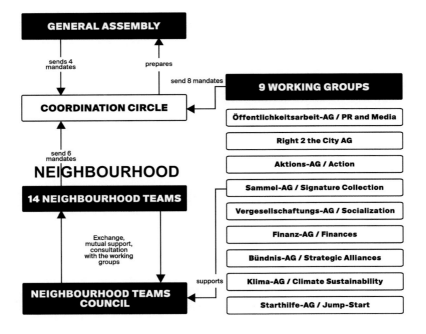

Figure 3.7 DWE's organisational structure
(*Source:* DWE)

After DWE's General Assembly decides that DWE will organise another referendum, I ask activists how they feel about it, looking back on the huge effort they put into organising the first one. Their responses are mostly stories of joyful persistence. T.'s eyes sparkle when he recalls how, the first time he was hanging out posters, he knocked over the glue bucket and had to scrape all the glue off the pavement with his bare hands. K. got anxious when, after knocking on a stranger's door for the very first time, he was shouted at and accused of being a Communist – but the next person offered him tea and biscuits. A. tells me, somewhat apologetically, that she is 'almost happy' at the thought of doing it all over again.

7

The Berliner Albert Einstein voted 'Yes' in the expropriation referendum. The physicist was a vocal supporter of the 1926 referendum to expropriate the property of the former ruling houses without monetary compensation (Figure 3.8). The petition for the referendum (*Volksbegehren*) was organised jointly by

Figure 3.8 Poster for the 1926 referendum to expropriate the property of the former ruling houses (Translation: "Not a penny for the princes! Let them apply for unemployment benefits!")
(*Source:* Wikipedia/Creative Commons)

the Social Democrats (SPD) and the Communist Party (KPD), but support was unexpectedly high in the stronghold regions of the liberal and centrist parties. More than 12.5 million people signed the petition.

The principle of lobbying existed long before the term was invented. The wealthy use their wealth to secure support from the politics. In 1926, an association of former princes (*Vereinigung Deutscher Hofkammern*) allied with the conservative parties and launched an aggressive campaign to counter the expropriation referendum. The lobbyists spread misinformation, claiming that the referendum wanted to abolish private property altogether rather than curb aristocratic wealth. President Paul von Hindenburg abandoned all pretence of political neutrality: the official anti-referendum posters quoted his words describing expropriation as 'gross ingratitude' (*groben Undank*) to the monarchy.

Arguing that the expropriation of princes would require an amendment to the Constitution, President von Hindenburg changed the criteria for winning the referendum from a simple majority to a minimum 50 per cent voter turnout. Was this move legally justified? As usual with the law, there were valid arguments for and against. Perhaps if the initiative had called for socialisation (the idea was already present in Article 156 of the Weimar Constitution) rather than expropriation, it would have been possible to win through a simple majority.

In the expropriation referendum Einstein supported, more than 14 million people (96 per cent of all the referendum participants) voted in favour of expropriation. But the turnout was only 40 per cent – very high, considering the intense agitation for a boycott, but not high enough. Because of the additional legal hurdle introduced by the president, the referendum failed.

Reader, if you doubt whether DWE's project of the socialisation of housing will ever be realised, you are in the right place. This is the frontier of political realism. Can *demokratia* – the power of the people – still win out over the power of the wealthy? I honestly don't know. As a scholar, I have good reason to be sceptical. There is a lot of rigorous research that shows how effectively a wealthy few have harnessed the law to hijack the system of representative democracy, and how deeply their power advantage is ingrained in the system's self-perpetuating logic.[23]

As an activist, I believe that *believing in change* makes change possible. And as a scholar-activist, I am in the business of learning, with and from the movement that has visibly shifted the frontier of political realism, making the previously impossible real. And I have learned that in order to gain more power, you must first become aware of the power you already have – and use it.

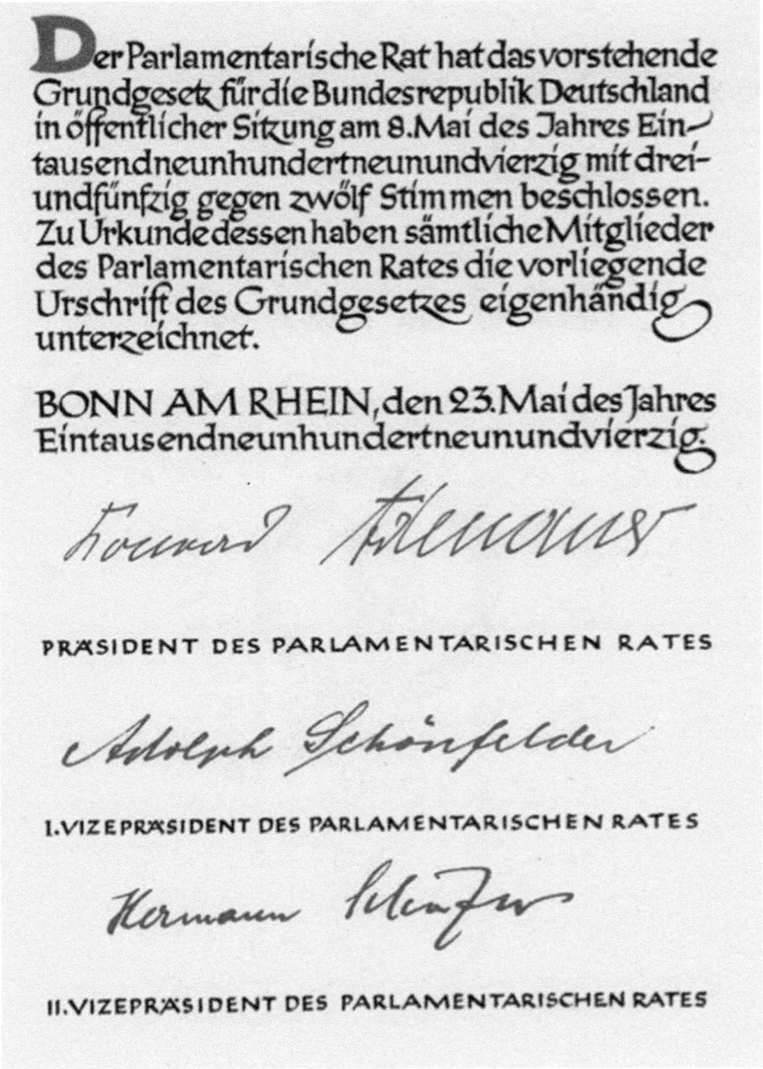

Der Parlamentarische Rat hat das vorstehende Grundgesetz für die Bundesrepublik Deutschland in öffentlicher Sitzung am 8. Mai des Jahres Eintausendneunhundertneunundvierzig mit dreiundfünfzig gegen zwölf Stimmen beschlossen. Zu Urkunde dessen haben sämtliche Mitglieder des Parlamentarischen Rates die vorliegende Urschrift des Grundgesetzes eigenhändig unterzeichnet.

BONN AM RHEIN, den 23. Mai des Jahres Eintausendneunhundertneunundvierzig.

PRÄSIDENT DES PARLAMENTARISCHEN RATES

I. VIZEPRÄSIDENT DES PARLAMENTARISCHEN RATES

II. VIZEPRÄSIDENT DES PARLAMENTARISCHEN RATES

Figure 4.1 Facsimile of the official signatures on the *Grundgesetz*

All state power derives from the people.
Article 20, *Grundgesetz für die Bundesrepublik Deutschland*

Ah, Grundgesetz, *yes,* Grundgesetz, *you keep invoking the* Grundgesetz. *Tell me, are you a communist?*
Franz-Josef Degenhart, German folksinger and
activist lawyer (from the song 'Interrogation
of a Conscientious Objector')

WHO CONSTITUTES POWER?

Checks and Balances

1

'What's your favourite article?'

I am chatty; Frau Schmidt is not. It's just the two of us in her small office. On her desk is a figurine of a bulldog nodding its head. Frau Schmidt doesn't nod. She looks at me seriously, questioningly. Maybe the final test is one of solemnity.

The first test, a few weeks ago, was the easiest – multiple choice about German culture, law and history. All questions available online for preparation.

After that came the real test. Excruciating. I've been posting a steady stream of papers to Frau Schmidt's desk for more than eighteen months. I have written a whole autobiography in stamped and certified forms, with long German words galore. I have arranged and rearranged my life in a yellow A4 folder, *in der richtigen Reihenfolge*: not in chronological order, but in the 'correct' order. By the end of the process, I could almost feel the pleasure of it.

This, now, is supposed to be the fun part.

'Frau Schmidt, do you have a favourite *Grundgesetz* article?'

I grin at her, playfully, placing my hand on the book in front of me. I brought my own copy. Preloved, with worn edges, and colourful index stickers poking out of it.

She looks at my hand, then at the book, then at the purple-yellow pin on my jacket. Our eyes meet. She smiles for a split second, then recalls herself to seriousness. She points at the black eagle on the cover of my book. I raise my hand.

Suddenly, it's not just the two of us in the room. I feel a powerful new presence: the State.

'I solemnly declare that I will respect the *Grundgesetz*, and the laws of the Federal Republic of Germany, and that I will refrain from doing anything that could harm it.'

When I finish this sentence, I am a German.

2

I am still Polish, too. My grandfather was raised by neighbours, because when he was 9 years old, the Nazi Gestapo arrested his mother. I grew up listening to Grandpa's occupation stories at bedtime: he had a great talent for deflecting trauma with humour. But when Grandpa visited me in Berlin, aged 85, he woke up in the middle of the night in terror. Outside, on the street, someone was yelling, '*Deutschland, Deutschland!*' It was during the 2014 FIFA World Cup.

My first German words were *halt!* (stop!) and *raus!* (get out!), which I had picked up from war movies. My school curriculum abounded in war books and war poems. When I moved to Germany, I realised that we hadn't been taught much about what had happened in Germany immediately after the Nazi defeat. What does a country do when it has murdered millions and wrecked the world, and wakes up, guilty, on a regular working Monday?

The country has to constitute itself anew. Or rather: its people must constitute themselves anew, as people – *the people* – and found a new state, by writing a new constitution. In post-war Germany, this was a daunting task. Most constitutions are written in moments of victory, from which their authors draw power and authority. In 1948, Germany still lay in ruins, humiliated by its excesses of power. The writers of the *Grundgesetz* had to derive their authority from this defeat.

Elisabeth Selbert, one of only four women among the sixty-five authors of the *Grundgesetz*, compared the launch of the

Figure 4.2 Opening meeting of the Parliamentary Council in Bonn,
1 September 1948
(*Source*: Federal Press Office [BPA])

Parliamentary Council tasked with writing it to a 'crematorium
ceremony'. The launch party was hosted by the Koenig
Zoological Research Museum in Bonn, with dead, stuffed
animals staring eerily at the jurists. 'It wasn't a fanfare for a
new beginning but the end of the end,' Selbert recalled[1]
(Figure 4.2).

The writers of the *Grundgesetz* (which means 'basic law' or,
literally, 'ground law') refrained from calling it a constitution,
mostly for fear that this would give fixed, legal status to the
partition of Germany into East and West. The *Grundgesetz* is
a constitution, nonetheless: a foundational utopia of the state.
Yet, as poetically pointed out by the jurist Heribert Prantl,
it was written as a mixture of genres. In some ways, the
Grundgesetz was like a school assignment that Germany, overseen
by the Allies, was required to complete, each of its 146 articles
another way of writing on the blackboard of history 'I will never
do it again'. It was also a 'letter of heartbreak', written by a
nation that didn't know whether it could still love itself, after all
it had done.[2]

Writing a constitution is an exercise of power – the constituent power, *verfassungsgebende Gewalt*. The German word *Gewalt* has a double meaning: power as faculty, the socially recognised authority, and power as violence, destructive force. In 1948, Germany's constituent power was acutely aware of its own violence. So when the authors of the *Grundgesetz* assumed the power to write the new future, they were neither triumphant nor naïvely optimistic. They were determined to learn from the experience of Nazi rule – and to implant in the *Grundgesetz* sufficient legal tools to prevent history from repeating itself

The rule of law offers two types of mechanism to prevent the abuse of power. Like most liberal constitutions, the *Grundgesetz* sets up systemic checks and balances. It divides state power into several branches – the legislative, the executive and the judiciary – that monitor and limit one another. The *Grundgesetz* also declares fundamental rights that guarantee a minimum standard for humanity. These rights are intended to protect people in their vulnerabilities, and help them to realise their freedom.

The *Grundgesetz* was written 'in German dirt, debris, and misery' – it was written with the humility that comes from humiliation.[3] This humility put the human at the centre of the nineteen fundamental rights (*Grundrechte*), even though the post-war years were politically and economically challenging.

[A]lmost one and a half million refugees were encamped in little Schleswig-Holstein alone, but a basic right to asylum ... was taken for granted ... The murder rate had risen to unprecedented heights in the insecure post-war years, but the abolition of the death penalty was written into the Grundgesetz *nonetheless. The new threat of war, the danger of espionage and attacks was palpable, but there was no argument whatsoever about the ban on torture.*[4]

Of all the fundamental rights included in the *Grundgesetz*, by far the most controversial was the clause 'Men and women shall have equal rights', inscribed in Article 3. When Elisabeth Selbert first proposed it, not even the other three women supported her. Friederike Nadig, Selbert's colleague from the SPD, worried that equal rights would destabilise the whole system: 'You cannot try to override or change the whole of family law; that would mean legal chaos.'[5]

Most of the men, on the other hand, didn't even take Selbert's proposition seriously. According to the minutes, they reacted 'with hilarity'.[6] Back then, a married woman in Germany was not allowed to open a bank account; men had a legal right to terminate their wives' job contracts to make them attend to their duties in the home. The Parliamentary Council voted down the equality clause three times.

Elisabeth Selbert was furious. Abandoning all convention, she became, in her own words, a 'travelling preacher' of women's rights. For several weeks, she travelled all over Germany giving public lectures (Figure 4.3). She spoke to journalists and to the wives of conservative politicians. Her message was precise. Her anger carried energy. Soon, the Parliamentary Council was flooded with letters of protest.

All the female MPs from all the West German federal states (with the exception of Bavaria) sent letters – as did 40,000 female metalworkers and the entire female population of Dörnigheim (a town in Hesse), among others. Women's organisations, and the media, further amplified these voices. By 18 January 1949, the Parliamentary Council had apparently transformed into an army of feminists. 'Men and women shall have equal rights' was voted into the *Grundgesetz* – unanimously.[7]

Today, the idea that men and women should have equal rights does not seem very controversial – unlike the right to socialisation, as inscribed in Article 15. In 1948, the opposite was true. Support for socialisation was fairly mainstream, and few would have dared to deny that economic power could – like any kind of power – be misused against democracy.

Figure 4.3 The statue of Elisabeth Selbert in Kassel
(*Source:* Wikimedia Commons)

3

'[P]rivate enterprise cannot be maintained in the age of democracy.' On 20 February 1933, the newly appointed chancellor Adolf Hitler laid out his vision to the twenty-five heads of German industry. The principle of entrepreneurial leadership (*Unternehmertum*) was close to that of *Führertum*, he said; the bosses' power should not be restrained by the need to negotiate salaries with trade unions. Without hedging, Hitler presented his plan to end parliamentary democracy and destroy the labour movement. Then he asked the business leaders for their financial contribution.

'The [financial] sacrifice[s] would be so much easier ... to bear,' Hermann Göring, the President of the Reichstag continued, 'if it [industry] realised that the election of 5 March will surely be the last for the next ten years, probably even for the next hundred years.' The money poured in. A fund of 3 million Reichsmark was set up with large donations from Deutsche Bank, IG Farben (a conglomerate of six chemical and pharmaceutical firms including BASF, Bayer and Agfa) and AEG, among others.[8] Hitler kept his promises to his business donors: he banned free trade unions and ended democracy.

When the Parliamentary Council discussed inscribing Article 15 into the *Grundgesetz*, the memory of the enthusiastic support some industrial monopolists gave to Hitler was still fresh. And so, while the legal possibility of socialisation already existed in the Weimar Constitution, the threat of the 'misuse of economic power' was no longer an abstract possibility. And it wasn't only about their direct funding of Hitler: the fact that property, especially in heavy industry, was concentrated in the hands of a few monopolists was generally seen as having weakened the Weimar democracy – and enabling Hitler's war economy.[9]

As far as general debates about political economy were concerned, liberalism was still largely considered discredited by the crash of 1929/1930. The consequences of this crash, as well as the unequal distribution of wealth, were seen as key reasons for the Nazi Party's popularity with the masses.

In their party manifesto of 1947, the Christian Democrats (CDU) postulated *Gemeinwirtschaft* as 'an economic and social constitution that responds to people's rights and dignity, serves their spiritual and material growth, and secures an internal and external peace'[10] (Figure 4.4). For the Social Democrats (SPD), socialisation was one of the key points of their economic programme – a first step in the transition towards a socialist economy. Thanks to the support of these two major parties, clauses enabling socialisation had already been included in the newly passed state constitutions of Hesse, Bavaria and Rhineland-Palatinate.

Figure 4.4 'CDU fights for the Gemeinwirtschaft'; this 1947 poster shows that the Christian Democrats stood for a socialisation and solidarity economy
(*Source:* Wikimedia Commons)

There was also the broader political context: the power and organisational capacity of the labour movement. In November 1948, more than 9 million people – almost 80 per cent of the entire workforce – participated in a twenty-four-hour general strike in Bizonia (the British and American occupation zones combined). The strike was in response to the steep rise in food prices, which had been deregulated after the currency reform. This strike – the biggest in German history – effectively forced the CDU chancellor, Ludwig Erhardt, to change course, away from free market liberalism and towards a so-called 'social economy'.

For all these reasons, the intense disputes over socialisation within the Parliamentary Council were, for the most part, not a question of if, but of how. The differences between the parties concerned issues of compensation – the CDU didn't want social-isation without compensation, while the SPD wanted to make sure compensation of a merely nominal value was possible – and the mode of implementation, namely, whether it should be done via legislation or via an administrative act.

In the final wording, a compromise between the proponents of a *Gemeinwirtschaft* and its liberal opponents, Article 15 states:

> *Land, natural resources and means of production may, for the pur-pose of socialisation (*Vergesellschaftung), *be transferred to public ownership* (Gemeineigentum) *or other forms of solidarity economy* (Gemeinwirtschaft) *by a law that determines the nature and extent of compensation. With respect to such compensation the third and fourth sentences of paragraph (3) of Article 14 shall apply* mutatis mutandis.[11]

What does this mean in practice? First, socialization is a standa-lone fundamental right – that's why it has its own Article in the *Grundgesetz*. It is *not* a form of limitation on individual property rights, all of which are specified in Article 14. But socialisation stands apart from all the other fundamental rights in that it does not apply to individuals. It is a 'fundamental social right' (*soziales Grundrecht*): a collective right, or a legally enabled collect-ive possibility. The purpose of socialisation is 'not to limit the formal freedom of the few (owners), but to extend the substan-tial freedom of the many (non-owners)'.[12] This freedom of the many justifies expropriating a significant share of relevant resources from private enterprises.

Secondly, socialisation is a purpose in its own right. While it may indeed curb misuses of economic power and the monopol-isation of property, the real meaning of socialisation is affirma-tive, and lies in developing forms of solidarity economy: *Gemeinwirtschaft*. *Gemeinwirtschaft* strives for both fair distribution and democratic management of resources, which, for this dual purpose, can be withdrawn from the profit-oriented logic of the market. However, as a tool for democratising the economy, it cannot be implemented via an administrative act, only through legislation.

Thirdly, socialisation demands compensation – yet because its aim is to withdraw resources from the logic of the market, the compensation would likely be below market value. Ultimately, Article 15 is an expression of the constitutional principle of economic neutrality. The task of the *Grundgesetz* is not to uphold or prescribe a particular economic system (such as capitalism), but to ensure that fundamental rights are protected within whatever economic system the society might choose.

In 1948, the dread of relapsing into authoritarianism was strong. The members of the Parliamentary Council wanted to err on the side of caution. And so, in addition to the 'standard' constitutional tools, such as fundamental rights and systemic checks and balances, they introduced new formal tricks that would protect democracy from excesses of power. For example, they gave fundamental rights a 'pre-political' and 'supra-legal' status. This means that all fundamental rights – including the right to socialisation – are put 'rhetorically and legally before the actual existence of the Federal Republic as a political entity'.[13]

Another legal innovation to protect democracy is a special 'eternity clause' (*Ewigkeitsklausel*). It ensures that the precise wording of two articles – Article 1 and Article 20 – can never be changed. Article 1 declares human dignity inviolable. Article 20 asserts that '[a]ll state power derives from the people', and that the Federal Republic of Germany is 'a democratic and social federal state'.

4

What does 'a democratic and social federal state' really mean? When the different political factions within the Parliamentary Council finally agreed, after many long and heated debates, on the exact wording of all the Articles, their words were subjected to more long, heated debates among the jurists, who interpreted them in different, and sometimes even contradictory, ways.

The word 'social' in the phrase 'a democratic and social federal state' was the subject of one such debate, which became one of the most important for the interpretation of the *Grundgesetz*. Commonly referred to as 'the Forsthoff–Abendroth controversy', this debate played out in the mid-1950s between two prominent commentators of the *Grundgesetz*: Ernst Forsthoff and Wolfgang Abendroth.[14]

In German public law, the Forsthoff–Abendroth controversy is the equivalent of the legendary 1971 boxing match between Muhammad Ali and Joe Frazier – the fight of the century. Both jurists were heavyweight champions. Each of the contestants' new tricks made history in their respective disciplines. And the public was as excited by the game as by the politics behind it. Ernst Forsthoff, like Joe Frazier, was a representative of the pro-war establishment. Wolfgang Abendroth, like Muhammad Ali, was an activist – a socialist of the Frankfurt School who was open about the fact that he brought his political convictions with him into the ring. The two jurists were almost peers, but their careers had taken very different paths.

Ernst Forsthoff had had an impressive career. He became professor of public law at the University of Frankfurt in 1933, at the age of just 31. His predecessor in the role was Herman Heller, who, as a social democrat and a Jew, had been forced to flee Nazi Germany. However, Forsthoff was not an opportunist. His views remained strikingly consistent: he disliked pluralism and constitutional democracy before, during and after Hitler. In the early 1930s, he criticised the Weimar Constitution, saying it weakened the state by endorsing party competition and democratic control.

Wolfgang Abendroth, on the other hand, praised democratic control – and waited a lot longer for his career to blossom. In 1933, the Nazis deprived him of his licence to practise law. He worked instead as a legal advisor to opposition figures, until he was arrested in 1937 by the Gestapo and charged with high treason. After four years of imprisonment, Abendroth was forcibly conscripted into the 999th division, a penal military unit serving in occupied Greece. There, he helped to set up an anti-fascist cell before deserting to the Greek People's Liberation Army.

Forsthoff eulogised war. For him, war was a vehicle for fusing the authoritarian state with the Aryan folk. Just as the Nazis were taking power, Forsthoff published *Der totale Staat* ('The Total State'). The book praised 'legitimate authoritarianism' for finally superseding the constitutional state, with its self-critical distinction between the law and the people.[15] Hitler's 'great purge ... served to eliminate all those who could no longer be tolerated as foreigners and enemies'.[16] The 'qualitative total state' would be based on Führer, state and the Aryan folk.

In 1944, Abendroth was captured and imprisoned by the British, and spent two years in British internment camps. These included the Wilton Park re-education centre, set up in one such camp by a German Jewish émigré, Heinz Wilton, and run like an academic campus. Resistance fighters, political leaders and academics came to talk to former Nazi soldiers 'as partners' about the future of German democracy.[17] It was breathtakingly democratic.

Forsthoff was not a soldier; he was an academic. After 1945, he rejected calls for self-criticism over his support for the Nazi regime. He responded to them with an aphorism by Ernst Jünger: 'He who interprets himself sinks below his [own] level.'[18] In any case, Forsthoff was not a political activist; he was only a jurist. His defenders argued that he joined the Nazi Party 'relatively late', in 1937.[19] He endorsed the Nazi regime, but made critical points where he felt it was necessary. And so, while the 'denazification' committee initially classified him as 'incriminated', his case was soon dropped.

Back in Germany, Abendroth was finally able to relaunch his career. In 1947, he was appointed a judge in Potsdam and, in 1948, Professor of Public Law at the Friedrich Schiller University of Jena. However, his career soon stalled again – again, on account of his convictions. Potsdam and Jena were now in East Germany. Abendroth was a member of the Social Democrats (SPD). But in 1946, the East German government dissolved the SPD, and tried to force its members to join the Socialist Unity Party of Germany (*Sozialistische Einheitspartei Deutschlands*, SED). Abendroth resisted this, and in 1948 he fled to the West. In his resignation letter to the university, he spoke out against the dissolution of political pluralism in the German Democratic Republic.

Forsthoff, once he had officially been cleared of the political accusations against him, continued his impressive career. He became a professor of public law at the University of Heidelberg. In his works, he criticised the Nazi regime – but not for its moral atrocities. As far as Forsthoff was concerned, the downfall of Nazi Germany was the consequence of procedural failures. Hitler had failed to protect the authority of the state from the influence of the people. The 'total state' had been totally derailed because it had listened to the people. For Forsthoff, even the Third Reich was too democratic.[20]

Meanwhile, Abendroth kept getting into trouble. Just as he had opposed the banning of the SPD in East Germany, in 1956 he opposed the banning of the Communist Party (KPD) in the Federal Republic, which he again saw as the dismantling of Germany's pluralism. After his death, his most eminent student, Jürgen Habermas, described him as 'a partisan professor in the land of followers' (Figure 4.5).

Figure 4.5 Wolfgang Abendroth by Zersetzer.com
(*Source:* Creative Commons)

Forsthoff and Abendroth fought out their differences over the *Grundgesetz* in public. Forsthoff was one of its most vigorous critics. He worried that, like the Weimar Constitution, the *Grundgesetz* weakened the state by giving too much control both to political parties and to the people. Abendroth, however, considered the *Grundgesetz* to be quite a success. He had his favourite articles: Article 15, which allows for socialisation, and Article 20. And so, to defend the term 'social state' in Article 20, he confronted Forsthoff in the ring.

Ding ding! The bell rings. The gloves are off – the fight begins. Forsthoff leans in, putting his full weight behind his first blow. The jab is aimed at Article 20. He wants to rid 'a democratic and social federal state' of the word 'social'. But his punch lands on a high guard – an eternity clause protects Article 20 from any changes.

Abendroth responds with an uppercut: Article 28 speaks of a 'democratic and social rule of law'. But Forsthoff's right hook is relentless. He claims the word 'social' has no legal meaning. He keeps on punching: the 'social rule of law' is a contradiction in terms; the rule of law depends on full separation from society! The public gasps – Abendroth is on the ropes. But soon they realise this is just a trick, a rope-a-dope to wear out his opponent.

Abendroth comes roaring back with a hard left hook. But Forsthoff is prepared. Everyone knows Abendroth is a southpaw. Forsthoff throws a cross to the body, packed with the weight of his credentials. It was he who introduced the idea of an 'existential minimum' (*Daseinvorsorge*) to German legal thought, back in 1938. He endorses public services, but he won't allow the people to mess with the state and make their own decisions. It looks as if Abendroth is cornered.

But look at this nimble footwork! Abendroth pivots and dashes to deliver a full-frontal blow: the 'social rule of law' in Article 20 is a constitutional call to extend democracy into society. The word 'social' doesn't only mean welfare rights. The word 'social' also implies the democratic right to participation (*Teilhabe*) in shaping the society. Bam – Forsthoff hits the ground.

Is it a knockout? The referee starts counting. The Constitutional
Court confirms: Article 20 is a 'guiding principle' of the
Grundgesetz. The 'democratic and social state' is a valid legal
concept that empowers the democratic constituency to shape
society.[21] The audience roars with delight. Eight – nine – ten.

Abendroth won in the ring of public law. The Constitutional
Court's understanding of the word 'social' in Article 20 aligned
with his. Abendroth used legal arguments to dodge the fist of a
centralised state with the nimble footwork of democracy, the
push and pull of people's competing interests. He saw democracy as a regulated conflict through which a diverse society
approximates decisions that aim at least to be *fair enough*
for everyone.

To him, Article 15 gave society a constitutional ticket for
making democratic decisions about the economy – and for
shaping society *together*, beyond individual rights. 'If Article
15 were to be removed,' he once responded to the lawyers who
speculated that Article 15 had become 'obsolete' – 'Article 20's
definition of the Federal Republic of Germany as a social state
would become a thinly veiled lie.'[22]

Within German constitutional law, the legal status of the
'social state' is well affirmed and fixed. But Abendroth's victory
with Forsthoff didn't end history; no victory ever does.
As Abendroth was exiting the ring in triumph, the wind of
history blew the outer ropes away.

Suddenly, the whole world is the ring. Forsthoff, with his
state-strong fist, and Abendroth, with his democratic footwork,
stare at each other in disbelief. Then they look up. High above
them, they see a new creature hovering out of reach: the
Jabberwock. The referee announces the arrival of globalisation.

5

'To our misfortune, we won!' Lech Wałęsa, an electrician and
Nobel Peace Prize laureate, had a talent for casual prophecy. Like
any prophet, he didn't always know the exact meaning of his
words. But he was right.

Wałęsa lacked formal education, but he was a political artisan. He had intuition. He sensed that Solidarność's landslide victory in Poland's first free elections, in June 1989, was not simply checkmate. Rather, it shifted the game to a new and wholly unfamiliar terrain: the globalised West. Here, there were forces completely beyond Solidarność's control – and they turned out to be much less predictable, at least to Solidarność, than even those of the Soviet Union.

Solidarność lost twice. Each time, it lost even though it had won: and, each time, it was the democratisation of the economy at stake. First, Solidarność lost against the authoritarian Polish state, backed by the Soviet Union. And the second time, Solidarność lost against Poland's international creditors, backed by the International Monetary Fund (IMF) and the World Bank.

The first defeat was violent and spectacular. This was when the extra-constitutional military junta declared the movement illegal, on 13 December 1981. The announcement of martial law was timed to coincide with the national congress of Solidarność delegates in Gdańsk. Conveniently, the movement's leaders could all be arrested simultaneously, at their hotels.

Martial law was introduced for two reasons: Poland's deepening economic crisis, and mass support for Solidarność's plan for overcoming this crisis. In October 1981, with membership at a peak of 10 million, Solidarność ratified its official political programme known as 'The Self-Governing Republic' (*Samorządna Rzeczpospolita*). One of its key concepts was socialisation (*uspołecznienie*).

To Solidarność, the word 'socialisation' had a double meaning. On the one hand, it meant broad popular participation in political decisions, including decisions about the economy:

> *Society must be able to organise itself in such a way as to ensure a just distribution of the nation's material and spiritual wealth and a blossoming of all creative forces. We seek a true socialisation of our government and state administration. For this reason, our objective is a self-governing Poland ... This is why we demand social control over the government's anti-crisis measures.*[23]

On the other hand, socialisation entailed participatory management of publicly owned enterprises and their assets. This was a key element in Solidarność's plan for managing the crisis democratically:

A new economic structure must be built. In the organisation of the economy, the basic unit will be a collectively managed social enterprise, represented by a workers' council and led by a director who shall be appointed with the council's help and subject to recall by the council.

Before it was declared illegal, Solidarność managed to translate some of its postulates for 'socialising' public enterprises into new legislation.

The law on the self-government of workers in a state enterprise, passed by the Polish parliament on 25 September 1981, was remarkable not only because of its content (introducing elements of participatory management), but also because of the democratic process of negotiating the law, which was unprecedented in the authoritarian Polish People's Republic.

The most dramatic point in the legislation process was 'the rebellion in the parliament' on 24 September 1981. For the first time in history, MPs of the Polish United Worker's Party (*Polska Zjednoczona Partia Robotnicza*, PZPR) refused to follow their party leadership, instead backing the version of the law negotiated with Solidarność.[24]

But while Solidarność was still debating the compromises made in the legislative process, the military was already preparing 'Operation Fir', the coordinated arrest of the Solidarność leadership after the declaration of martial law. Solidarność was outlawed until April 1989. Its activists were violently persecuted, and the rank-and-file membership shrank by 75 per cent.

The second defeat of Solidarność was more discreet. Its violence, which I experienced as screams outside my window in Łódź, leaked into crime and poverty statistics, but was drowned out in public by the clamorous cheers of victory. To be fair, Solidarność's victory was not a trivial thing. The 1989 elections

Figure 4.6 Electoral poster of Solidarność on a Warsaw tram
(*Source:* Wojciech Druszcz)

were the first free elections in the whole of the Eastern Bloc. Wonderfully, Solidarność's new government restored to Poland the civil liberties of Western democracy (Figure 4.6).

Then Solidarność implemented shock therapy: an economic programme that was the exact opposite of the self-governing republic, and violated most of the social protections promised in the Round Table agreements. When people reacted with strikes and mass protests, the new government ignored them, effectively betraying its own social base. The spirit of solidarity was defeated.

'We believe that people's power is a principle that we do not have the right to abandon', states Solidarność's famous programme.[25] So why did the leaders of Solidarność abandon this principle once they were in power?

There are many explanations. Politically, the eight years in which Solidarność was outlawed effectively undid its mass character, cutting the leadership off from the base. Ideologically, Chicago-school neoliberalism became the new global zeitgeist,

with envoys of Thatcherism and Reaganomics screaming promises of freedom. Materially, the new government was presented
with two options: the carrots of neoliberal freedom, or the stick
of foreign debt if Solidarność refused to eat them.

When Solidarność came to power, Poland was 46.1 billion US
dollars in debt. Until 1989, Poland's creditors in the Paris Club used
the debt to exert control over the authoritarian regime, justifying
it with their concern for democracy. The infamous empty shelves
in Polish shops were partly the consequence of export clauses
attached to loans, which required repayment in products and
raw materials. Rising food prices – the main reason for the protests
that led to the formation of Solidarność – were partly the result of
creditors 'hammering hard at the Polish pricing system', which
was designed to keep food prices below market levels.[26]

Solidarność was a democratic movement that peacefully and
democratically overthrew the authoritarian regime that had put
the country in debt. Shouldn't this have been a good enough
reason for creditors to give Poland's new government some debt
relief? But the IMF took a hard line. In the United States, George
H. W. Bush, after congratulating Solidarność on its victory,
made clear that the new government was still responsible for
repaying the old debt. Poland was caught in a debt trap.[27]

Earlier, at the Round Table Talks, several options for the
Polish economy had been discussed. Beyond the 'self-governing
republic' and Thatcher-style neoliberalism, there was also significant support for the 'Swedish model': a welfare state
working closely with the unions.[28] Now, with inflation at
600 per cent, something had to be done, fast. Chain-smoking in
stuffy meeting rooms, the activists-turned-politicians slowly
began to grasp the extent of their misfortune: their democratically won freedom was haunted by economic dependency.

A bullwhip cracks. A mustang whinnies. Jeffrey Sachs, the
'Indiana Jones of economics', has arrived in Warsaw. Sachs is by
no means an activist: 'I'm not a naïve do-gooder,' he explained to
The New York Times. He is an independent expert. With his 'out-
spoken views and a penchant for Third World countries', he is a
travelling salesman of economic 'shock therapy'. He has already

recommended it to Bolivia and, parallel to his engagement in Poland, he is also advising Venezuela and Mexico.[29]

Sachs is a 34-year-old Harvard professor who has never held any position in government. He is, however, extremely well-connected in Washington, DC and in the IMF. His magic touch softens the creditors, who promise debt relief – but only if the government adopts a hard line against its people. Sachs emboldens the new government to go against the Solidarność programme; they can pull it off, he says, precisely because people trust them. In any case, they don't have much choice.

Sachs drafts his economic programme for Poland in a single night. On my fourth birthday, the parliament passes the legislation that will force Poland to go cold turkey with deregulation, austerity and privatisation. Politically, the implementation of shock therapy relies on a flight from democracy, and pushing ahead as fast as possible, against the protests of the people.[30] As a result, Solidarność splits internally and engages in a destructive inner conflict. It loses the 1993 elections to members of the former communist party.

But wasn't it all worth it in the end? The shock therapy worked, didn't it? That depends on your perspective. If you consider only abstract economic benchmarks, it was indeed a success. Since 1992, Poland's GDP has grown steadily. But GDP only measures the overall market value of goods and services bought and sold within an economy. Once you break these numbers down into stories, the picture becomes more complicated.

Throughout the whole of the 1990s, more than a third of the population of Poland lived below the poverty line. The group that benefited most from the rapid privatisation of industry was the elites of the communist regime. A study conducted in June 1993 showed that 67 per cent of the presidents of management boards of privatised enterprises were already directors before privatisation.[31] The social anger at Solidarność's betrayal was captured by right-wing authoritarianism.[32] Salaries in Poland are still among the lowest in Europe.[33] The average tenant in Warsaw spends more than half of their income on rent.[34] Since 2004, 2.5 million Poles have left Poland. Me too.

6

All state power derives from the people. When I swear on the
Grundgesetz, I become part of 'the people'. From now on, constitutionally speaking, Germany's state power also derives from
me. Saying it to myself out loud, holding a certificate of natural-
isation that smells of fresh ink, it feels somewhat grandiose. But
then I catch myself. Do I have citizen impostor syndrome?
Or maybe we all have an impostor syndrome: we-the-people,
unsure whether the state power we constitute really is ours
to use?

Contemporary Western democracy has been hollowed out; it
is a 'democracy without *demos*'.[35] This was the diagnosis of Peter
Mair, an Irish political scientist who devoted his life to a com-
parative analysis of political systems in Europe. The word 'democracy' literally means 'rule of the people'; it assumes that
people can exercise agency on the system that governs them.
In theory, this idea is still widely endorsed by the political elites.
In practice, however, political parties have long since abandoned
the premise on which they were founded: representing the
interest of their electorates.

Mair's analysis shows that the programmatic gap between
mainstream political parties – even ones that are formally in
opposition to each other, like the SPD and CDU – is now much
smaller than the gap between any of these parties and their own
voters. From the 1980s onwards, parties have abandoned the
task of political representation, and have gradually withdrawn
from the realm of the civil society. Instead of being *responsive* to
their voters, the politicians claim to be *responsible* with regard to
the economic system.[36]

Almost all mainstream parties still declare their commit-
ment to democracy. Yet when it comes to economic policy,
representing the interests of voters is dismissed as populism.
This anti-democratic rhetoric is being justified by the fiscal
crisis and the growing indebtedness of the contemporary
state. Economic policy has widely been handed over to central
banks and international financial institutions, which prioritise

the wellbeing of the financial markets while being described as 'independent'.

As pointed out by the economic sociologist Wolfgang Streeck, the 'independence' of these financial institutions does not mean they are free of political agendas – only that they are free of democratic accountability.[37] Sheltered from democratic procedures that would evaluate them based on the effects of their policies on a political community, they can neutralise democracy by overruling voters' preferences. This is what happened in Poland in 1989 – or in Greece in 2015, when, during the country's government-debt crisis, the international creditors effectively blackmailed the Tsipras government into ignoring the results of the referendum, in which people had rejected the shock-therapy-like bailout conditions driven by harsh austerity.

In theory, economic globalisation and egalitarian democracy have a common value denominator: freedom. However, while democracy and the rule of law both pursue the normative ideal of the 'free and equal subject', the globalised economic system lays claim to freedom while perpetuating inequality. Moreover, the supposedly 'neutral' financial experts limit the notion of freedom to individuals. When a single person, driven by their self-interest, makes an economic decision, this is perceived as the cornerstone of the free market. Yet as soon as people make an interest-driven decision together – act on their *shared* economic interest, using democratic procedures – their freedom is narrated as a threat to the economy.

This limiting of collective freedom appears rather *unfree*. More importantly, though, the claim that limiting democratic control of the economy is done in the name of individual freedom is factually incorrect. As pointed out by the Nobel Prize-winning economist Elinor Ostrom, even most 'regular' companies are in fact collective endeavours.[38] Financial markets, on the other hand, are run exclusively by extremely powerful collective entities: banks, investment funds and corporations.

As creatures of the financial market, corporations are de facto large, socially uprooted shareholders' collectives. Their

enormous power does not derive from anyone's individual freedom. It derives from a coordinated and pooled interest, a form of
oligopoly. This oligopoly has gradually developed into what
Louis Brandeis, a future US Supreme Court Justice, was already
calling, in 1913, 'financial oligarchy'.

More than a century later, the existence of the financial oligarchy is impossible to deny. Between 2020 and 2023, the richest
1 per cent grabbed almost two-thirds of all the world's new
wealth – almost twice the amount shared by the other 99 per
cent of humankind. If the world's richest ten men 'were to lose
99.999 percent of their wealth tomorrow, they would still be
richer than 99 percent of all the people on this planet'.[39]
It would be naïve to assume that such a massive accumulation
of wealth could occur without political coordination. And it
would be facile to imagine that this coordination happens at
various secret gatherings, as conspiracy theories would have it.
How do the super-rich communicate in order to coordinate their
interests politically?

The super-rich communicate through money. Jürgen
Habermas calls money a 'steering medium' of the contemporary
economy: a communicative tool that coordinates the interest-
based action of economic agents without the need for language-
based conversation. Money 'has the properties of a code by
means of which information can be transmitted from sender
to receiver'. Because such communication is 'de-linguistified'
and uprooted from the social context, it is also sheltered from
political questioning of deliberative democracy.[40]

Now, it would be all-too-easy to dismiss Habermas's
theory as a de facto conspiracy theory wrapped in the sort
of intellectualised metaphor typical of German philosophy – were
it not for the fact that the US Supreme Court, for example, has
actively endorsed the vision of reality that Habermas critiques.

In January 2010, in *Citizens United v. Federal Election Commission*,
the US Supreme Court ruled against government bans on the
corporate funding of electoral committees. In this way, the
Supreme Court effectively permitted corporate money to over-
whelm the electoral process. Most importantly, though, in

justifying this decision, the Court equated the ban on corporate spending with a limitation on free speech.

Free speech is a civil liberty protected by the First Amendment to the United States Constitution. In the justification of the majority opinion, Justice Kennedy argued that funding a political campaign with money amassed on the market is a form of political speech. He also stated that the civil right to free speech should not be limited to 'natural persons' (humans), or even apportioned differently between humans and corporations.[41] Effectively, the US Supreme Court empowered a legal fiction that assumes both economic and political equality between a human person and a corporation. For isn't a human person – a teacher from Michigan, for example – free to spend as much money on campaign funding as, for example, Google or Amazon?

Concealed behind the fiction of a 'legal person', a corporation – a super-powerful, socially detached collective of shareholders – can pursue its group interest while narrating this as individual freedom. At the same time, when a democratic constituency – a collective of citizens territorially rooted in a community – openly and transparently pools people's interests based on the basic needs of the individuals (everyone's individual need for housing, for example), the supposedly 'independent' financial agencies narrate this as a threat to individual freedom.

While money needs neither language nor parliamentary democracy to serve as a means of communication, it does need something else: the law. Neither money nor financial markets could exist if they weren't anchored in the law. Money, too, is a legal fiction: a hundred-dollar banknote is a worthless piece of paper unless the law declares it valuable, and most financial wealth doesn't have even this much materiality. The connection between money and power is forged by private law.

But neither private nor international law can exist without the nation states that back them. And the Western liberal ideal of the rule of law *still* commits the nation states to the rules of parliamentary democracy. Thus, the rule of law – and especially the public law that *still* upholds some principles of egalitarian democracy – becomes the only meaningful interface where democratic people's power has any chance to counter the financial oligarchy.

In the US context, the *Citizens United* decision is so poignant (and scary) because it legally dismantles we-the-people as a political community of real humans. And it doesn't do it to protect other living creatures, or even our planet as a living ecosystem. No. We-the-people must give up our privileged political status to feed the fictional Jabberwock with even more power.

However, if the corporate Jabberwock were to attempt to assume the political status of a human being under the terms of the German *Grundgesetz*, you would very soon hear the clip-clopping of hooves as Immanuel Kant comes galloping in on his great Holsteiner horse. His categorical imperative, legally inscribed in the *Grundgesetz*, explicitly protects *human* dignity and rights.

As Kant enters the Federal Constitutional Court to make his stand, he sees, sitting on the benches, the sixty-five mothers and fathers of the *Grundgesetz*. Through their special eternity clause, they remain ever-present, ensuring that their wording of Article 1 and Article 20 can never be changed.

Human dignity shall be inviolable. The Federal Republic of Germany is a *democratic* and *social* federal state. All state power derives from *the people*.

7

The Berliner Walter Benjamin argued that time, in politics, is not always linear. Sometimes, suddenly, the 'now-time' (*Jetztzeit*) ripens with the energy of past struggles. Short-circuited by the power of the present, the past may blast open the continuum of history and take a 'tiger leap' into the future.[42] This might be happening now to Article 15.

Over the course of history, many people have devoted their energy to making socialisation and *Gemeinwirtschaft* possible. Article 15 carries in itself the triumphant people's power of the German Revolution, the persistent will for self-determination of the workers' movement, and also the humble strength of the mothers and fathers of the *Grundgesetz*, who took on the responsibility of learning from one of history's darkest periods.

After this, for almost seventy years, the notion of socialisation was forgotten. History is written by the victors, and they tend to edit out elements of the past that do not fit their victorious narrative. Some victors even have the boldness to claim both past and future, announcing – like Francis Fukuyama after the collapse of the Eastern Bloc – that all history has ended.

But history does not cease just because someone wants it to. The past, albeit dormant, remains a resource for the future. According to Benjamin, the emancipatory energy of the past is stored in the materiality of our cities. By virtue of their diversity, cities never succumb to any one, single story. But the past also dwells within the law, which – *because* it is conservative by nature – has protected the legal possibility of socialisation from the changing winds of politics.

For Benjamin, the past ripens to its full meaning not when it is simply retrieved or memorialised, but when it transforms itself by short-circuiting on the here-and-now. This, too, is the story of Article 15. When the Parliamentary Council was writing the *Grundgesetz*, the threat of the 'misuse of economic power against democracy' was thought of only within state boundaries. But even then, the mothers and fathers of the *Grundgesetz* considered it a danger. They intuited that economic power – like any form of institutionalised power – had to be checked and held in balance by other powers.

With economic globalisation, we are increasingly confronted with the need to impose checks and balances on economic power operating globally. If it is true that the state is a Goliath that, if not democratically restricted, may crush individual freedom, the same is true for the corporate Jabberwock.

In most democratic states, however, the people lack legal tools to enable them to counterbalance economic power. With Article 15, the mothers and fathers of the *Grundgesetz* achieved a double constitutional innovation. First, they extended the idea of democratic checks and balances to include the economy. They gave the state a legal tool for limiting economic power if it starts to run wild. And they opened the way for the people to control the economy by democratic means. Secondly, they extended the notion of fundamental rights from the individual to society, thus allowing free and equal subjects to be *free together*.

Even with Article 15, it would not be easy to counter the power of the corporate Jabberwock. One could certainly expect the 'independent' financial institutions to mobilise in order to disable the idea of economic democracy. In January 2019, when the first polls showed Berliners overwhelmingly supporting socialisation, the international credit rating agency Moody's threatened to downgrade Berlin's international rating if the city went ahead with socialisation.[43] The threat is wrapped up in a one-page 'report' that contains no meaningful legal or economic analysis. But it fulfilled its role: it produced headlines that projected socialisation as an 'irresponsible' desire of the people.

But what if assuming democratic control to fix the system's perversion is the most *responsible* thing we-the-people can do? By now, it is mainstream knowledge that the global financial system misuses its power: we know this from *Financial Times* articles and *Netflix* movies as much as from academic publications and activist statements. To know that something is harmful and not to act on this knowledge, or to keep replaying the same set of strategies when we know full well that they didn't work before: is this a *responsible* thing to do?

With Article 15, the *Grundgesetz* offers a powerful tool for curbing the misuses of corporate power responsibly, within the bounds of the democratic system. And while the global financial system would inevitably rebel against this solution, Germany is the world's fourth largest economy and arguably the most powerful country in Europe. It has enough power to back a democratic decision taken by its own people.

Many times in the past, Germany has leveraged its economic power to prevent other democratic constituencies – in Greece and Poland, for example – from exploring alternatives to austerity and privatisation. The socialisation of housing in Berlin could therefore send a paradigm-shifting signal to the entire global economy that an alternative is indeed possible, and worth exploring.

All state power derives from the people. As I swear on the *Grundgesetz*, I suddenly have a flashback to my grandfather's moment of terror. When I get home, my daughter looks at my certificate and asks me what a citizen *does*. The present short-circuits: suddenly, I feel on me the eyes of both history and the future.

(5)

Figure 5.1 Hermannplatz 2050: An Artwork by Gosia Zmysłowska
(*Source:* Gosia Zmysłowska)

According to the Grundgesetz, the present economic and social order is a possible order, but it is by no means the only possible order.
The Federal Constitutional Court of Germany (BVerfG 1954, 4,7)

I no longer want to draw utopias 'in principio' but absolutely palpable utopias that stand with both feet on the ground.
Bruno Taut, Berliner, Chief Architect of GEHAG (a non-profit housing and building company established in 1924 and privatised in 2007)

BERLIN IS THE GREATEST EXTRAVAGANZA

Sexy and Solidaristic

1

What does the future look like? Eager to fall into a Wonderland of innovation, I attend *FUTURE PropTech London 2019*: 'the world's largest and most cutting-edge property technology show'. The event advertising promises more than 100 'thought leaders from around the globe' who will talk about the 'macro-economic challenges facing the real-estate industry and how technology is overcoming them'. The nine 'key urban challenges' mentioned in the programme include 'Tech-Enabled Brokerage' and 'Solving the Housing Crisis'. I am curious.

Judging by the venue, the future looks like a touristified food market in an arbitrary European city. Everyone is wearing a suit, and access to the venue is strictly limited – but the food in the hall is being served from food trucks to give it an 'urban' feel. I circulate between the stands to learn about the latest innovations. One of them is an 'unrivalled' CCTV technology for landlords. I can see myself on the screen; it's following me. At another stand, a woman presents a 'revolution in coliving': a scheme to 'increase your revenue' by renting apartments to groups of roommates who are organised via an app. Notwithstanding all the tech, it seems to me that the biggest innovation occurring here is at the level of language.

I write down some PropTech keywords on my branded notepad. At lunch break, waiting in line to collect my tacos, I tell the people around me about Berlin's latest PropTech innovation. 'It's a smart platform for the optimal allocation of property,' I say. One man seems particularly interested. He asks me about the technology we use.

'We crowdsource for legal innovation,' I reply. 'The technology we use is called 15GG. It creates loads of value for the key urban stakeholders.' I smile at him, and at myself for making a private joke: GG is the standard abbreviation of *Grundgesetz*. The man writes '15GG' on the back of my Cambridge business card. He asks if I would potentially be interested in business-to-business collaboration. 'We work with a whole range of urban stakeholders,' I assure him.

Back in Berlin, I call my friend Patrizia, who works in start-up funding. She is an enthusiastic supporter of socialisation, and was one of the thousands of individuals who contributed personal funds to DWE's crowdfunding campaign. Together, we draft a pitch.

In Berlin, innovative young players have been disrupting existing markets to break the mould and create a better future. The PropTech market is ripe for this acceleration, with DWE perfectly placed to employ swarm intelligence for the most efficient resource allocation. Using a decentralised toolkit and state-of-the-art 15GG technology, DWE transforms property markets to create exponential added value for key urban stakeholders. Say yes to the revolution in the sharing economy!

A genuine innovation can speak any language.

2

Bruno Taut was a pioneer of PropTech. Coming from the Bauhaus tradition, Taut believed that new ways of thinking about property – as a social arrangement facilitated by modern technology – could genuinely transform society. So when my Cambridge students visit Berlin on a research trip, I take them to Bruno Taut's Carl Legien Estate in Prenzlauer Berg, the one

Figure 5.2 Felix's apartment at Carl Legien Estate
(*Source:* Karsten Buch)

I discovered on my very first walk around my neighbourhood. This UNESCO World Heritage site provides homes for nearly 3,000 Berliners, including my friend Felix. As twenty-four students, divided into groups of three, consecutively marvel at the way natural light flows through his living room on a grey March morning, Felix tells us how he enjoyed spending all the COVID-19 lockdowns here (Figure 5.2). Indeed, when Taut was building the estate in 1928, he specifically factored epidemics – the main consideration back then being tuberculosis – into his design.

Taut designed spaces, not just buildings. He considered 'light, air and the sun' to be the creators of good architecture. The Carl Legien Estate features spacious green courtyards intended for sunbathing, outdoor exercise and community gardening. To give city-dwellers the feeling of being in nature, Taut reversed the traditional floor plan of the urban tenement. Here, the living rooms, as well as the bedrooms, overlook the green courtyards. The kitchens and bathrooms face the street.

Figure 5.3 Colourful loggias at Carl Legien Estate
(*Source:* Karsten Buch)

Taut's smart design was geared towards quality of life. Every apartment has a loggia (a roofed balcony) that extends the living space in summer. The smallest apartments have the biggest loggias. Every loggia has built-in storage that doubles as a fridge in winter, when people stock up for Christmas.

'We don't want to build any more joyless houses', Taut wrote in a manifesto he signed along with other Bauhaus architects.[1] He was a functionalist, but considered joy one of the important functions to which architecture must cater. His colour-coding of doors, balconies and windows – in saturated yellow, red and blue – is deliberately playful, intended to lift people's spirits (Figure 5.3). The large corner windows, emblematic for

Bauhaus design, increase the amount of daylight while also adding interest to the façade.

Bruno Taut's joyful apartments were affordable by design. Taut was committed to solving the housing crisis, which was why Berlin's visionary city planner Martin Wagner appointed him as the chief architect of GEHAG. This was an innovative non-profit company, set up by Berlin's various trade unions and cooperatives to build affordable housing on a massive scale. Legally, GEHAG was a cross between a building society and a joint-stock company that catered exclusively to non-profit shareholders. It had its own subsidiary developer (Deutsche Bauhütte), to avoid wasting resources on commercial profit margins.

Taut's high standards did not compromise either the speed with which the apartments were built or their affordability. The 1,149 apartments of Carl Legien Estate were completed in just two years. All of them had modern bathrooms and furnished kitchens – a major improvement on the general living standards of the time. The estate's communal spaces included two laundry areas, several shops and a café. For some critics, making such beautiful housing so affordable was controversial. Taut's housing was 'too nice for the working classes', they said.[2] Between its launch in 1924 and its takeover by the Nazis in 1933, GEHAG built around 17,000 apartments.

GEHAG was privatised in 1998. In 2007, it was acquired by Deutsche Wohnen, and Deutsche Wohnen merged with Vonovia in 2021. Deutsche Wohnen lays claim to Taut's legacy in its corporate logo by including a horseshoe – a direct reference to the 'Horseshoe Estate' in Britz, awarded UNESCO World Heritage status in 2008 (see Figure 5.4).

In 2022, Anne Kockelkorn, an architecture professor from Ghent University who lives in Berlin, conducted research to find out whether corporate landlords were doing justice to Taut's institutional and architectural legacy.[3] Corporate landlords have access to huge amounts of capital, as well as modern technologies. Kockelkorn wanted to know whether these resources had translated into actual innovation.

Figure 5.4 Bruno Taut's Horseshoe Estate in Berlin-Britz built by GEHAG
The estate is listed as a UNESCO World Heritage Site. Currently, it is owned
by Deutsche Wohnen.
(*Source:* A. Savin, Wikipedia)

Firstly, she assessed 'Marienufer', a sixteen-hectare site advertised in Deutsche Wohnen's 2020 shareholder magazine as the
'living spaces of tomorrow'. The project is managed by a PropTech
platform 'for the control and optimisation of financial flows in the
development of real estate'. As noted by Kockelkorn, the project's
rendering on the website 'aestheticises the scheme's attempt to
eliminate all non-commodifiable collective space'. Unlike Taut's
lavish courtyards, green spaces at Marienufer are minimal.

Contrary to what the district authorities proposed in their
local development plan, the Marienufer estate has no central
neighbourhood square and no social amenities. The urban front
of the project is a series of parking spaces. Also, while the
architectural rendering presented floor-to-ceiling glazing, implying plenty of natural light, the resulting project features much
smaller windows set in plain beige render.

Figure 5.5 'Architecture of financialisation': A housing project by Vonovia in Alt-Tempelhof, completed in 2021
(*Source:* Anne Kockelkorn)

After Marienufer, Kockelkorn visited an unnamed housing project in Alt-Tempelhof, completed by Vonovia in 2021. From what she describes, no one can criticise it as being too nice for the working classes. To begin with, the working classes can't afford it: the rent of €12 per square metre is the maximum legally allowed in this area. Secondly, it is not nice: Kockelkorn found that 'the simple shape, rough aesthetics and cost-saving construction processes are reminiscent of the minimum standard design of emergency shelters'[4] (Figure 5.5).

Kockelkorn concludes that the quality of architecture is closely linked to the institutional set-up. What Deutsche Wohnen and Vonovia build is 'an ideal city of financialisation', cost-optimised to maximise profit rather than comfort of living. In this respect, the architecture is functioning perfectly: in 2021, Deutsche Wohnen made a profit of €919 million, Vonovia €2.8 billion. A family living in a Vonovia apartment is paying an average of €195 per month just to cover the shareholders' dividends.[5]

Martin Wagner and Bruno Taut – the visionary architects and planners who effectively ran GEHAG – built their 'too nice' houses on standard civil service salaries. The managers of Deutsche Wohnen and Vonovia are undoubtedly well qualified – but not in housing or planning, only in 'asset management'. In 2021, the average annual salary paid out to the members of the Vonovia Management Board was €2.5 million. Vonovia's CEO, Rolf Buch, earned €4.2 million.[6]

Bruno Taut was a pragmatic idealist. He believed that in order to transform the system you have to aim as high as possible, while standing with both feet on the ground. To train himself to aim high, he would draw outlandish utopias. He considered this an important exercise: if you can't find the courage to 'go for it', even on paper, would you ever dare to transform the real world? Indeed, as soon as Taut was granted the authority to make decisions, he directed all his powers towards creating the 'absolutely palpable utopias' that are still among Berlin's best living spaces today.

As a pragmatic idealist, Taut believed that a good cause requires equally good marketing. In order to attract more attention to his housing projects, at the 1920 'New Building' exhibition he deliberately placed them beside his most fantastical drawings. His most far-out utopia – *The Alpine Architecture* (Figure 5.6) – was intended as a visual reminder that the resources wasted for the destruction of war could have been used to create something wonderful for people and the planet. 'And if one succeeded in directing these [destructive] forces into another, more beautiful channel', Taut wrote, between the First and Second World Wars, 'then the whole Earth would become like a good apartment'.[7]

3

At 104 years old, Karl-Heinz Peters was frail. But when he saw his life's work being destroyed, a powerful current of anger surged through his veins, right down to his fingertips. That's why, at 104 years old, Karl-Heinz Peters wrote a book. He typed

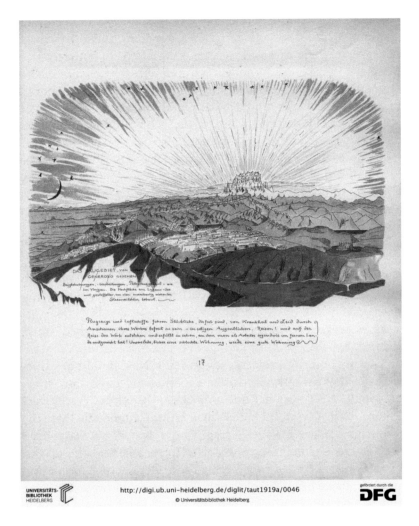

Figure 5.6 Alpine Architecture: An outlandish utopia by Bruno Taut

every word of it himself, his pale fingers trembling over the vintage keyboard. He titled it *From Public Interest to Private Profit: GEHAG, a Victim of Privatisation, and the Challenges for Alternative Housing Policy*. 'All the big names of the previous housing system are sitting on their pensions, doing nothing,' Peters told a journalist from the *Berliner Zeitung*. 'Someone had to stand up and intervene ... The basis for my book is anger.'[8]

The greatest piece of luck in Karl-Heinz Peters' long life was pulmonary tuberculosis. Having contracted it in 1938, he was classed as unfit for military service. Instead, he trained as a lawyer and worked in the management of the Reich chamber of commerce. Peters was grateful to have avoided being sent to the front by the Nazis, and after the war he swore to use his expertise to rebuild social democracy.

In 1949, Peters got an emergency call from the trade unions. GEHAG was being abolished. Like all trade union property, GEHAG was seized by Hitler in 1933. Consequently, after the war, the Allies classified it as a Nazi organisation, and proceeded to dismantle it. Peters describes GEHAG as 'a precious, broken vase' that lay in pieces on the carpet of history, the carpet itself divided up into Berlin's legally separated zones of occupation. Putting the pieces back together was a challenging task. GEHAG's archives had been bombed, its documents were missing and its properties were scattered across different jurisdictions. Peters deployed all his legal and managerial know-how. He also scoured West Berlin in search of other experts who would join him in his mission to save Taut's and Wagner's institutional legacy.[9]

It worked. GEHAG was relaunched in 1951. In 1953, Peters was appointed to direct it, which he continued to do until his retirement in 1978. He urged his employees in the letting department to invest in maintaining long-term relationships with tenants so they all felt truly at home. He made GEHAG participate in the International Building Exhibition. He personally convinced Bauhaus architect Walter Gropius to design an estate in Neukölln, negotiating the project with the then-mayor, Willy Brandt. Peters was willing to work with any political faction to make housing affordable. What he was not prepared to do was sell himself, or his dedication to the public interest, no matter who was making the offer.

Peters saved GEHAG more than once. In his book, he recalls a 1956 dinner invitation from Heinrich Plett, the chairman of

Neue Heimat, which was run by the trade unions and was, at the time, Germany's largest not-for-profit housing company. Plett wanted GEHAG to merge with Neue Heimat. He tried to convince Peters that GEHAG would benefit from Neue Heimat's 'self-financing system'. Peters suspected that this meant strategically utilising tax breaks to make deals with private business. 'When Plett told me, rather bluntly, that I could earn significantly more this way, I decided to leave his house,' Peters recalls.[10]

In 1982, Neue Heimat went down with a bang. The 'self-financing system' turned out to be a tool for corruption and speculative development. To enrich themselves, board members were awarding lucrative contracts to companies run by cronies. They drove Neue Heimat into debt, while also raising tenants' rents. In 1986, Neue Heimat – a company that owned 200,000 apartments – was privatised for the symbolic price of one German mark. This first transaction was legally reversed, but the housing stock was still sold off to private landlords.

The Neue Heimat scandal became an excuse to dismantle the entire system of not-for-profit affordable housing. In 1990, the federal government under Helmut Kohl abolished the legal concept of 'affordable housing as a public benefit' (*Wohngemeinnützigkeit*), as well as the tax benefits for not-for-profit housing companies. This effectively ended the long era of German state support for affordable housing.

Having fended off Neue Heimat, Karl-Heinz Peters lost GEHAG in an internal power struggle. Wolfgang Materne, who joined the board of GEHAG in 1978, opened one of the last meetings Peters attended by declaring, 'You are all too oriented towards the public good.' Even after Peters left, he continued to keep an eye on GEHAG from afar, as an expert in the Federal Association of Housing Cooperatives. And the more he saw, the angrier he got.

In 1993, Karl-Heinz Peters got angry because GEHAG issued some 'VIP funds' that offered huge tax advantages to a network of political cronies.

In 1998, Karl-Heinz Peters got angry because GEHAG was privatised. Bruno Taut's palpable utopias were flogged off at an average price of 30,000 marks (around €15,000) per apartment. A year later, Jürgen Klemann, a prominent CDU politician who helped to set the conditions of privatisation, became a member of the board of the privatised GEHAG.

After privatisation, Karl-Heinz Peters got angry so many times he lost count. The behaviour he considered to be the core of corruption – extracting collectively created value for private profit – had been elevated to an official business strategy. GEHAG fell prey to 'a swarm of locusts': private equity firms whose strategy is to jump on an under-priced company and suck maximum value out of it (in GEHAG's case, by splitting up the portfolio and selectively selling assets), then resell the company for a profit. Between 1998 and 2007, GEHAG was bought and sold five times – until it was eventually acquired by Deutsche Wohnen.

Deutsche Wohnen operates on a long-term strategy based on raising rents and neglecting maintenance. This was not one to soothe Karl-Heinz Peters' anger. Peters was outraged that Deutsche Wohnen was using Bruno Taut's flagship architecture to market itself, while building almost nothing of its own. Between 2014 and 2019, Deutsche Wohnen built fewer than 100 apartments in Berlin. Peters quotes a 2010 interview with the Deutsche Wohnen CEO Michael Zahn, who declared that new construction was simply 'not profitable enough', and that raising the rents provided a more stable perspective for securing shareholder revenue.[11]

At the age of 104, Karl-Heinz Peters realised that he would not be able to die peacefully unless he took a strong stand. In his book, he argues that housing needs to be organised in a func-tional *system*, and that this system needs to have rules that safeguard it from exploitation. Freeloading on collectively pro-duced value is a threat that can come both from within (as with *Neue Heimat*'s internal corruption) and without (as with the big finance preying on Berlin's collectively created and historically rooted housing system). In this respect, Peters' views were aligned with those of Elinor Ostrom, who argued that the over-use of shared resources happens both under private and under public ownership – it's a function of poor checks and balances in the system that governs these resources, not the form of owner-ship as such.

'In view of the current [housing] situation, the argument of "politically impossible" should be impossible to make.' This is the last sentence of Karl-Heinz Peters' book. After writing it, Peters died, aged 105, in 2017 – the birth year of Deutsche Wohnen & Co. enteignen, and of my daughter Mira.

4

In Germany, a doughnut without a hole is called a *Berliner*.

Mira finds it on our kitchen table, wrapped in a brown paper bag on which someone has scribbled 'EAT ME!'. She is sure it was not there a second ago. She ventures a taste. The filling has a curious flavour: plum jam, currywurst, rhubarb spritzer, falafel, pickles.

'Mum!' she exclaims, as I enter the kitchen. 'I'm opening up like a telescope!'

'That's great, darling,' I mumble. I only got up from my desk to make some more tea. I'm trying to figure out how to work my way into Chapter 4, part 4.

'Mum! You're lost in your head again!'

A wave of maternal guilt crashes on the shore of my con-sciousness. I look down, searching for Mira's face – and to my surprise, I find myself staring straight at her belly instead, which is sticking out of a T-shirt that no longer fits her. My gaze races up my daughter's body. She's so tall that her face hovers above mine. My guilt surges. Somehow, while I was busy playing with words, my daughter has shot up and outgrown me.

I'm not sure how to deal with it. I try to gather my thoughts, and bite into the half-eaten Berliner. From here on, things just get curiouser and curiouser. My body starts to shrink; it feels like being tickled. But Mira, who now looks like an adult, still has her child-like ability to normalise whatever life throws at her. She picks up my dress from the kitchen floor and puts it on.

She brings me some clothes from her wardrobe in exchange. Then she takes my hand and leads me out of the apartment.

Danziger Strasse is sun-drenched, lushly green and uncanny. After a while, I realise that what is puzzling me is the lack of noise. The usual hum of traffic is absent. Only two of the former six traffic lanes are left; very wide bike paths have taken over the rest. The cars are sweepingly silent. A sudden memory of a camping weekend in Brandenburg comes rushing back, and I notice that the city smells different. Behind me, a loud jangling jolts me back to the present: aha, the yellow caterpillar of the tram is gliding through the city as usual.

Mira tugs at my hand, and we run towards the stop. As people squeeze onto the 15 tram, the fresh breeze mixes with sweat, adrenaline and perfume. '*Scheisse!*' – a retiree in a leather jacket swears about the tram being late, *as usual*. An old lady in a priority seat is eating a buttercream gateau. The tram is turning; she manoeuvres the silver fork to prevent the cream from staining her pink tweed blazer. At the next stop, we squeeze up to make space for two men carrying a sofa. One of them is on the phone: his wife is divorcing him; he's moving to a smaller apartment. 'The twins are at the local school, so the AöR gave us extra points in the apartment allocation lottery. It's just two stops away; they can walk between our two places on their own!' Someone steps on my foot twice and doesn't apologise. I exhale. Curiouser or not, this is Berlin.

A horse is standing beside the ticket machine. A tall Italian gesticulates wildly, trying to explain to the ticket inspector that he forgot to buy a ticket the moment he saw the horse. '*Mamma mia, è il cavallo di Kant!**'

'*Ist mir egal.*'** The inspector remains unimpressed. 'This horse has a Deutschland-Ticket. Where's yours?'

'Mira, look!' I nudge my daughter. 'It's Kant's horse!'

'But where's Kant?'

'At home, in Königsberg. You see,' – I'm glad to be able to fall back on the comfort of old knowledge – 'Kant is obsessive about his routine. For him, freedom means he's not forced to move

---

* Mamma mia, this is Kant's horse!   ** I don't care.

anywhere. He wouldn't write anything otherwise. But as *The Critique of Pure Reason* became a late bestseller, Kant delegated his horse to travel with his ideas. That way, he is always free to stay.'

As I say this, a car whizzes past our tram. It's an electric convertible with a vintage feel: a recorded engine roar blasts from the external speakers. The car is driving itself, but on the front couch I recognise Elon Musk and Jeff Bezos. 'Fuck Berghain! Fuck Berlin!' they yell.

'Oh, fuck off to Mars!' a passenger with orange hair and a lightning bolt painted across his face shouts back at them through the tram window. 'Wow – these people are completely out of touch. Who are they? Who do they think they are?'

'Don't worry, it's just a hologram,' says an emo teenager, calming him down. 'They were a couple of businessmen who visited Berlin in the early 2020s. They threw such a spectacular tantrum when Sven wouldn't let them into Berghain that a local artist turned it into public art. They're sort of city mascots – a reminder that, in Berlin, no one is above anyone else.'

'For sure – *everyone* gets refused entry to Berghain. They turned me away, too!' The guy with the lightning-bolt make-up gives a melancholy sigh.

'You should come to Lichtenberg some time,' says a lady in her seventies. She has an East Berlin accent; her hair is as bright orange as his, only shorter. 'The best new-wave parties are in Kalinka.'

'I'm Ziggy.' He extends his hand to her.

'So am I,' she replies. 'Siggi, that is. Sigrid.' She pulls a string of fairy lights from her tote bag and wraps them around his body. '*Na, Kleiner*, this really suits you!'

'C'mon, people, don't you get tired of Berlin sometimes?' A suit-wearing guy stops rummaging through his backpack to join the conversation. 'This city is still so provincial compared to other metropolises, and so nonchalant about its imperfection. It has no ambitions for greatness!'

'DEAR PASSENGERS!' The voice of the tram driver blasts from the speakers. 'PLEASE MIND THE GAP BETWEEN THE TRAM AND THE PLATFORM EDGE – BUT DON'T LET THE GAP STOP YOU FROM GETTING ON BOARD!'

'Well, maybe Berlin has *different* ambitions,' Siggi replies. 'The ride is the riddle!'

'And of course I get tired of Berlin,' Ziggy nods energetically. 'Every evening, I get sooo tired, as one can only get tired from a day full of living. Berlin,' – Ziggy waves his hands in the air, as if to include all of us, the tram, the whole city – 'Berlin is the greatest extravaganza that one could imagine.'

The tram crosses the Oberbaum Bridge and heads towards Görlitzer Park – the tracks no longer end at Warschauer Strasse. I'm too short now to see the information poster in the tram, so Mira reads it to me. Like the Jubilee underground line in London, this tram line was opened to celebrate an anniversary: twenty years since the socialisation of housing in Berlin, the first successful use of Article 15 in German history. The socialisation of the energy networks followed soon afterwards. Fun fact: the Pirate Party's project to socialise hip sneaker stores – a joke that went viral – was rejected in the early stages, because it didn't fulfil the legal criteria for socialisation as defined by the Constitutional Court.

The jubilee tram route is called Berliner Freedom. It starts at the Carl Legien Estate in Prenzlauer Berg and ends at the Horseshoe Estate in Britz. Along the route, the tram passes the award-winning Wolfgang Abendroth Estate: using technology developed by a local start-up, a team of Berliner architects turned an abandoned office building into an ecologically sustainable coliving project.

As the tram approaches Hermannplatz, I spot a familiar face.

'Mira, it's Gem!' I am genuinely excited. 'Let's get off and see who they've become now!'

Speaking of Berliner Freedom: Gem, who uses the 'they' pronoun, has lived at least a dozen lives, and has excelled in all of them. I first met Gem when they were a recent graduate of an Ivy League university who had quit academia to become a birth assistant – a doula. In the scariest moment of my labour, Gem held back the walls of the universe and stopped them from crumbling. Never before had I realised that empathy can be physically palpable. In between guiding new Berliners into the world, Gem provides companionship to people who are dying. Gem has also recorded an album of electronic music and performed in a musical.

Lastly, Gem holds space for sex-positive parties. 'Holding space' is care-work jargon that describes a mixture of organisation, facilitation and empathetic presence. Sex-positive parties, for which Berlin of the early 2020s became world-famous, are orgies without a moral hangover: inclusive, consensual spaces where people freely celebrate their sexuality while respecting one another's boundaries.

'Birth, sex and death all require the same core skill,' Gem told me, back when I was soaking in the birthing tub. 'It's the willingness to embrace the whole human mess of living.'

'Hello!' Mira squeeze-hugs the person who first welcomed her into this world, in a public hospital in Kreuzberg. 'Who are you these days, Gem? Look – Mum has shrunk!' she says cheerfully.

'Well, if that's her thing ...!' Gem smiles at me, impressively unimpressed. 'I'm a conflict facilitator now, Mira – I work here.' They point to the old Karstadt building, which now has a lush green façade. The building is topped with a pink neon sign that says *AöR*. The bubbly dots above the 'ö' are effervescent, like a glass of pink champagne.

'Gem, did they name the whole institution just *AöR*?' I ask. 'The acronym for *Anstalt des öffentlichen Rechts*, an institution under public law?'

Gem nods. German administrative culture loves long names and quirky acronyms.

'But it's so unspecific!' I say. 'Can you name an institution "An Institution"?' It's like naming your dog "Dog".'

'Mum, come on, *you* should know!'Kids have a distinctive way of frowning at their parents when they think they're being a bit slow. 'The full name is *AöR Gemeingut Wohnen* ["Common Living: An Institution under Public Law"]. But it's too long, so everyone calls it *AöR* – like you did when DWE was first drafting the legislation to set it up. Don't you remember? There was no name, and no real thing, just some dry legal text. But you were all soooo excited about it! As if "an institution under public law" were the sexiest thing on the planet!'

'Berliners are kinky for democracy!' Gem winks and unzips their jacket. Right across their breasts there is a large inscription:

AöRM *aber* SEXY

'What does the crossed-out M stand for?' Mira asks.

'Oh, of course, you wouldn't remember!' I explain: 'In the early 2000s, Berlin had this mayor called Klaus Wowereit.'

'Wasn't he the first openly queer politician?'

'Yeah, but he also privatised public stuff like crazy, and he had that whole spiel about romanticising austerity. He advertised Berlin as "poor but sexy" – *ARM aber SEXY.*'

'But that was well before you were born, kiddo. Now, it's SEXY AND SOLIDARISTIC.' Gem pulls us in through the revolving door. 'Come on, girls, I'll show you around!'[12]

5

In the big entrance hall of the AöR building, the main wall has been turned into a vertical hydroponic garden in the shape of Berlin. Each district is made up of different kinds of plants.

'It's more or less complete now,' says Gem. 'This map was created by people from the Treptow district council so we could visualise our progress on modernising our housing stock to make it environmentally sustainable. First they just laid out a hydroponic map of Treptow, but after the pictures went viral we decided to make a bigger one, covering the whole of Berlin. When we started, it was more or less an empty frame; we add a plant whenever all our buildings in a block of streets have been properly insulated to reduce heating costs and CO_2 emissions. At some point, the AöR secured a package deal for upgrading properties, and after that it all moved really fast.'

'Nice!' Mira strokes the leaves of one of the plants low down on the wall. 'When I move out of Mum's place, can I get one of these nice apartments in Britz? There's so much going on there now!'

'Well, you can if you're lucky! Our system allocates the apartments blindly, through a weighted lottery. You won't get extra points just because you want to move out of your mum's place. But when your mum gets old and frail' – Gem winks at me – 'if you want to live nearby, to support her, you might get extra points for that.'

'What else do you get extra points for?'

'For legitimate needs. For example, if a couple separates but are sharing custody of their children, the system gives them extra points for a given area, so they can stay close to each other, and to their children's school. Extra points are also granted to people on low incomes, or those who may face discrimination on the housing market for whatever reason. The system also automatically awards extra points to people from demographics that are severely underrepresented in particular areas, to preserve the Berlin mix.'

'How can I apply?' Mira persists. 'If this is a lottery, I still have a chance, right? Even without the extra points?'

'Correct! All you need to do is fill out an online form with all your data. You don't need to provide any paperwork until you're actually offered an apartment. People can apply as individuals, families, or flat-shares. The algorithm allocates available apartments every two weeks. For each apartment, it generates a ranked list of five applicants. The first person on the list is immediately invited to view the apartment. If they don't take it, we invite the second person, and so on. If you reject three apartments, you're excluded from the lottery for six months.'

'And what if you already have an apartment, but you need a bigger one – because you want to live with other people, for example?'

'You can participate in the lottery, but the system can also help you find a swap. We offer incentives for people to swap a bigger apartment for a smaller one – when their kids move out, for example. They can stay in their neighbourhood, if that's what they want, and we cover their moving costs. And they'll be paying less rent, because the price per square metre is the same for all the properties.'

'Does the algorithm also decide which shops to allocate to the ground floor of a building, if a space becomes available?' I ask.

'Oh, no – the people decide that.' Gem laughs. 'So there are always new reasons for my job to exist.'

'What do you mean?' Mira is curious.

'Well, at all the different levels of the AöR structure (Figure 5.7), people have the option to make democratic decisions. The system is set up as a mixture of direct and representative democracy: you can participate, but you don't have to. Many people do want to participate, though, which means they have to figure out a solution together. Often, the path to a socially sustainable decision means going through a short but intense phase of conflict. My team's role is to facilitate those conflicts, to help people understand each other's needs and emotional responses and find a constructive solution. Come on up – I'll show you our facilitation spaces.'

We take the lift to the top floor. Gem shows us into a large, bright room with a circle of twenty chairs.

'The circles can be up to fifty people, depending on the issue and the stakeholders,' Gem explains. 'This week we've got a relatively small group from Zehlendorf. The local estate council is in conflict over what should be on the ground floor of one of the buildings: a kindergarten or a supermarket. There are some real characters in the group, like a female writer who claims that children's noise makes her ill, and a businessman who starts each meeting by saying that our whole AöR ought to be privatised immediately. He's really fighting for the kindergarten though; he has three kids.'

'And how do they figure it out? In the end, it'll be either the supermarket or kindergarten; you won't satisfy them all.'

'True, although we do always look at the broader context as well: what spaces are available in the neighbourhood, and what's needed. Sometimes there are other possibilities that we didn't see at first glance. And sometimes some people don't get what they hoped for, but at least they understand why. These are the smaller conflicts, though. Personally, what I enjoy most are the annual meetings of the Governing Council.'

'How so?'

'The Governing Council was deliberately set up in such a way that no group has an easy majority with which it can dominate the others. These checks and balances are a key part of AöR's

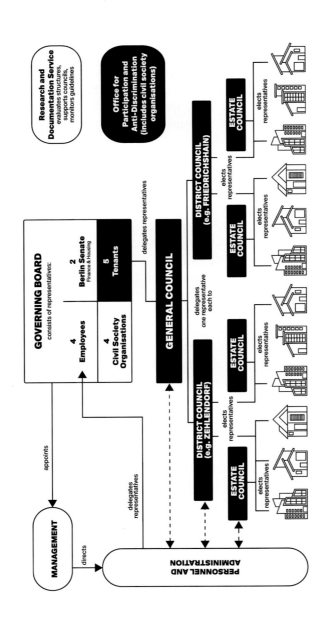

Figure 5.7 Organisational structure of the AöR, a democratic institution that would manage socialised housing
(*Source*: DWE)

institutional design; we learnt a lot from the failures of GEHAG and Neue Heimat. So on the Governing Council you have four representatives of the tenant body, four representatives of the AöR administration, two representatives of the Berlin Senate – the senators responsible for housing and finance – and four directly elected representatives of Berlin's civil society organisations.'

'So you also have people on the Council who don't live in AöR apartments?'

'We own so much housing that our decisions impact the whole city, not just the people who live in our homes. It's important that all Berliners are able to have a say in how we operate. That was always the problem with cooperatives: they're great, but all too often they turn into closed shops that usually privilege their own members.'

'Wow! And you facilitate the conflicts between all these different factions? The tenants, the citizens, the politicians and the administration?'

'At this level, we don't call it conflict facilitation – it's our standard decision-making process. At first, many people were worried that if no faction had a majority on the Governing Council, no one would have the proper authority to make decisions, and people would just waste time on endless deliberation.'

'Don't they?' I ask. 'I've been involved in lots of participative processes that were mostly a waste of time. Often because, after all the discussions, someone just took an arbitrary decision anyway.'

'Our decisions are taken through a streamlined, iterative process. The process is oriented towards concrete results, which makes it a bit similar to design thinking. Also, we always begin with a phase in which we challenge our assumptions about how we define the problem. Our process is also significantly different from design thinking, though, because it's guided by the principles of democracy. The solution is most sustainable if we manage to get everyone on board with it.'

'So what does the Governing Council decide on?'

'Each January, there's a week-long residential session during which the Governing Council works out the plan for the coming

year. In preparation for the residential session, our research
service, in collaboration with civil society organisations, reports
back on what worked and what didn't in the previous year. They
also analyse current demographic and ecological factors that
need to be considered. Some representatives of the research
service and the civil society organisations also participate in
the residential session. The civil society representatives also act
as watchdogs; they prepare a public report after the meeting.
But they don't watch from the outside. They sit in the circle with
us and participate in the discussions. It is very easy to criticise
someone else's decisions if you haven't experienced the democratic heat in which they were forged.'

'Aren't the senators afraid to participate in a conflict that's
being reported on?' I ask. 'They need to preserve their public
image, after all!'

'The observers have a mandate to report on the various phases
of the process and the ways in which we arrive at decisions, but
not on people's individual responses. That way, the process is
transparent to the public, but the detail remains confidential.
For the process to be productive, people must feel safe to express
themselves honestly in the heat of a high-stakes conflict, without worrying about social media reactions, or comments being
taken out of the context.'

'I see ... And what does the plan for the year include?'

'The most important part is updating the guidelines derived
from the AöR Constitution.'

'AöR Constitution? Like the *Grundgesetz*?' Mira asks.

I jump in. 'I think I know. It's like a little *Grundgesetz* for a
single institution. When DWE first drafted the law to set up the
AöR, they insisted on legislating checks and balances within the
AöR structures, to make sure it can't be taken over by the
interests of any one group.'

'Exactly!' Gem confirms, and smiles. 'You know, in working
here I've learnt that democracy is not that different from birth,
death and sex.'

'Because it demands that we embrace the whole human mess
of living?' Knowing Gem, I could see this metaphor coming.

'Yes! They all expose us to the whole spectrum of human nature: our high and low motivations, our struggle for control, our fears and our needs. But there are some important differences. Birth and death are challenging because when we go through them we are essentially alone. Sex and democracy are challenging because they inevitably expose us to other people. We rely on others to help us realise our freedom and desires.'

'So you're saying that democracy is kind of like Berlin's sex-positive parties?' I smile, trying to visualise this metaphor.

'Well, to make either of them work, you have to stick to the same three basic rules. The first is that you have to create a space where everyone feels welcome just for who they are.'

Mira interrupts: 'The second rule is probably that you have to have rules. Mum *always* says that.' It seems not all my efforts at parenting were wasted. 'Some basic rules allow people to seek their freedom without hurting each other.'

'OK, I think I know what's third.' I smile at Gem. 'We've been talking about it in DWE since the very beginning.'

'What is it, Mum?'

'Protesting against what you don't want isn't enough. With democracy – as with sex – you also have to allow yourself to say what you *do* want. You might need to negotiate with others to see if they want it, too – but until you say your wishes out loud, you'll never know.'

'Oh, yesss.' Gem is glowing. 'To get to a better future, you first have to shamelessly, publicly want it.'

6

After discussing sex, it's time to talk about money – the last taboo of polite society. How much would it cost to socialise 240,000 apartments currently owned by corporate landlords? Article 15 prescribes that expropriation for the purpose of socialisation must be compensated. As always with the legal matters, the wording is important: the cost of socialisation is 'compensation', not a 'price'. It is not defined by the market (though market prices might be used as a reference point), but by the law.

The legal aim of the compensation is 'establishing an equitable balance between the public interest and the interests of those affected'.[13] By referring to the 'public interest', the law requires the legislator to consider non-monetary interests when calculating the monetary value of the compensation. Even in relation to standard expropriations based on Article 14 (equivalent to compulsory purchase orders in the United Kingdom, or eminent domain in the United States), the Constitutional Court has ruled that: '[A] rigid compensation based solely on market value is alien to the *Grundgesetz*.'[14]

How does the principle of balancing interests compare with the supply-and-demand logic of a market price? When I first moved to Berlin, I discovered a small winery in Prenzlauer Berg that provides a concrete example. Every evening, a bartender puts a selection of fine wines on the counter, and each guest is given a glass. The bartender invites the guests to serve themselves, asking them only to (try to) remember how many glasses they drank in the course of the evening. On leaving, the guests are asked to pay as much as they would like to, considering the wine they drank, the overall worth of the experience, and the amount they feel *able* to pay.

The customers balance their financial interests (what they can afford) against the interests of the winery (whose wine they have drunk), and other values they consider important. The value component gives the customers' decision an essentially political character. If a customer primarily values the principle of solidarity, she might end up paying a different amount from a customer who values saving. Customers also differ in the estimation of their own interests. The wine is not being sold at market price; instead, the bar is entrusting its customers with the task of 'legislating' appropriate compensation.

A corporation, the public interest, and a legislator walk into a bar. 'I can drink 240,000 glasses and still walk straight,' the corporation boasts. 'I feel you,' the public interest responds. 'Every time you do it,

I'm the one who loses their balance.' But it's the legislator who provides the real punchline.

The decision on compensation has to be made by a legislator. Every socialisation requires a separate law that, among other things, defines how the compensation should be calculated. The legislator's decision is political, but not arbitrary – it is bound by the law.

To facilitate the legislator's decision, the Expert Commission on socialisation, which was set up by the Berlin Senate after the successful DWE referendum, has carefully considered the legal framework for compensation. The majority of the Commission's experts agreed that the compensation cannot be based primarily on market value. This is because the constitutional purpose of Article 15 is to withdraw resources from the logic of the market in order to create a pocket of *Gemeinwirtschaft*, solidarity economy.

With the view on the purpose of Article 15, the majority of the Commission's experts agreed on three possible models for calculating the compensation. The first model highlights that the compensation must naturally be limited by its fiscal affordability. With this, the experts disprove some critics' concerns that socialisation would blow Berlin's budget: the cost would legally be limited to what Berlin can afford without neglecting other spheres of public interest.

The second model endorsed by the majority of the Commission's experts proposes that compensation be calculated as the maximum amount of a loan that the new housing institution (AöR) could afford to pay back with the rental income – under the proviso that the rents must be kept affordable. This proposition is very close to the 'fair rents model' for calculating the compensation, as originally proposed by DWE.[15]

The third model is largely hypothetical. The strongest possible way of limiting corporate landlords' property rights without expropriation is compulsory management (*Wohnraumzwangsbewirtschaftung*). This has a historical precedent: such a law was introduced in West Germany in 1953 to alleviate the housing shortage. It gave local authorities the right freely to assign people to vacant flats, including those belonging to private individuals. It also strictly regulated rents. A legislator could calculate compensation as a hypothetical market value of corporate-owned housing in such circumstances.

In addition to the majority opinion, the Socialisation Commission's final report also includes a dissenting view. Three of the thirteen experts insist that the balancing procedure should be based on the market value. The dissenting voters do agree that *something* must be deducted from the market value to account for the public interest. What can legitimately be deducted? The Commission's experts agree that the compensation would have to cover the original purchase price of the apartments, as well as increases in value directly created by the corporations (by investment in modernisation, for example). However, they also all agree that the corporations do not need to be compensated for increases in value that they have not merited, such as those resulting from changes in zoning regulations.

In prioritising public interest over market value, the majority of the Commission's experts closely follow the constitutional purpose of Article 15: to create a *Gemeinwirtschaft*, a pocket of an alternative economic system that is not driven by profit and growth. According to the *Grundgesetz*, the present economic order is 'by no means the only possible order', as the Constitutional Court once put it. By continuing to insist on prioritising the market price, the people behind the minority vote are effectively imposing market-economy rules on Article 15, which was explicitly created to escape these rules. This is not just a question of logic: it is a political battle being fought on the basis of the law.[16]

This small legal battle is part of a bigger political question on the agenda today, namely: what is the purpose of our economy? Kate Raworth, an Oxford-based economist, suggests that we can no longer afford to fetishise linear economic growth: it is destroying our planet, and does not serve people well. Instead, Raworth proposes a circular model that is similar in many ways to *Gemeinwirtschaft*. She calls it 'doughnut economics'. She

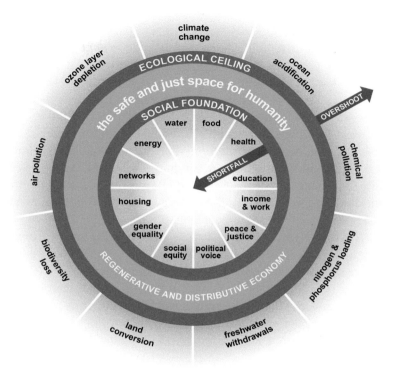

Figure 5.8 'Doughnut economics' by Kate Raworth

visualises it as a doughnut, the outer edge of which marks the ecological limit beyond which growth-oriented activity harms the planet, for example through excessive pollution or the overuse of resources. The hole inside the doughnut represents the proportion of people falling short of life's essentials, such as food or housing (Figure 5.8). Raworth argues that all the human capacity for innovation should be directed not towards growth, but towards reaching the 'sweet spot of humanity': keeping our planet alive, and closing up the hole in the doughnut.

Without denying the need for innovation: Berliners have always loved their doughnuts without a hole.

7

After leaving the AöR, Mira and I take a walk along the Landwehr Canal in Kreuzberg, passing the hospital in which she was born. This is our ritual walk, and everything is the same as always. The cool river breeze puffs around tiny, warm clouds of weed smoke. The expats are drinking oatmilk lattes, the natives are drinking Schultheiss, and the Prenzlauer Berg mothers like me are drinking ayran. A Turkish-looking youth is recording authentic German hip-hop, while the German '*Pfand* lady' is collecting deposit bottles. People are talking to one another, and people are talking to themselves. There are perils to big-city freedom: some people go bonkers.

As we approach the hospital, a woman calls to us from a bench, in Polish. She looks strange. In her segmented yellow puffer coat, she reminds me of a giant caterpillar.

'Who are you?' she asks us, in Polish. She is smoking a hookah, and she blows the smoke right into our faces.

'Well, who are *you*?' Mira is quick-witted.

'I am who I am. I was a tram driver, but now I'm retired. I'm just visiting, anyway. They're the locals!' She points to the two friends sharing the bench with her. 'You lot need to do something. This city is losing its democratic muchness!'

The guy on her left looks mad as a hatter. He has a wild white hairdo, and introduces himself as Einstein. Their other friend looks gentle. His name is Benjamin. Behind his round Windsor glasses, he seems as shy as a rabbit.

'We need to make use of the city's muchness in order to save it.' Benjamin speaks softly, so we all lean in to listen. 'The law knows what it wants. All we have to do is hold the sword of the law together.'

'Your law can make the muchness much muchier,' the tram lady says, matter-of-factly.

As much as I agree, I am also confused. 'But is all this muchness just a dream? I don't want to be impolite, but sometimes I worry I have dreamt you all up.'

'No, Mum, I get it!' Mira cuts in. 'Berlin's muchness is not a dream. It's a *memory*. Some people want us to believe we're dreaming a Wonderland. But this city was real.'

'This city *is* real,' Einstein nods. 'And the Jabberwock is nothing but a legal fiction. But the dangers of fictions are real. You must expropriate the Jabberwock on Vergesellschaftung Day.'

'Oh dear! Oh dear! We shall be late!' Benjamin pulls a watch out of his waistcoat pocket; the watch shows fifteen o'clock. 'Quick!' He jumps up. 'Follow the law!'

'But wait!' says the Polish tram lady. 'This has to be a decision you all make together. Because when you go out to expropriate the Jabberwock on Vergesellschaftung Day, you must hold the sword of the law together. And after that, you must hold the city's muchness together.'

'Expropriate the Jabberwock? On Vergesellschaftung Day? But when will Vergesellschaftung Day happen?' I am getting impatient.

Einstein takes Benjamin's watch and dips it in my ayran. 'Stupid girl! If you knew Time as well as I do, you would know that the distinction between past, present and future is just a stubborn illusion. Vergesellschaftung Day is happening now.'

'She's *not* stupid!' My daughter stands up to Einstein in my defence.

'Who are you, then?' The tram lady's question drifts towards us on a cloud of hookah smoke.

Mira takes my hand. Our fingers sticky with doughnut glaze, we answer proudly, in unison:

'*Ich bin ein Berliner.*'

Figure 6.1 Waiting for the tram
(*Source:* Eva Schneuwly / DWE)

Democracy is a system that guarantees we will not be governed better than we deserve.

Jacek Kuroń, the 'godfather of the Polish opposition', one of the political strategists of *Solidarność*

Sometimes we drug ourselves with dreams of new ideas. The head will save us. The brain alone will set us free.

But there are no new ideas still waiting in the wings to save us ... There are only old and forgotten ones, new combinations, extrapolations and recognitions from within ourselves, along with the renewed courage to try them out.

For there are no new ideas. There are only new ways of making them felt.

Audre Lorde, activist and poet, Berliner from 1984 to 1992

THE RULE OF LAW IS
HAVING A MIDLIFE CRISIS

Shadow and Difference

1

'You won, ...'

I can hear the comma after 'won'. I hope I can hold out. I tense the back of my throat and silently count to ten. I count in German, to stay prepared. He wants to finish but he's resisting the conclusion.

'... but it could be dangerous for the rule of law.'

I agree with him. Which is why I disagree with him. I wonder how I can pack this into a soundbite. Dry air teases my tonsils. It's a quarter past ten; Berlin's nightlife is just beginning. I stare at the bookshelf and notice my shadow falling across my legal literature.

'Herr Steiner, the rule of law is having a midlife crisis. The rule of law must embrace its own contradictions.'

I put down the phone and cough my eyeballs out. This is the sixteenth interview I've given today, the day after DWE won its first referendum. Though, naturally, we don't call it 'the first referendum' just yet. I am elated and exhausted.

This morning, I was the first patient in the doctor's surgery. I have been sick for two weeks, and have been ignoring my sickness. For the last three months, it's been all hands on deck. Because of the overwhelming media interest, I've joined the press team, and am serving temporarily as one of the DWE's spokespeople. I went to bed at 3 a.m. I cannot speak. I must speak.

'What's the strongest cough suppressant available in Germany? Could I get that? In large quantities, please.'

The doctor shakes my hand as he hands me the prescription. 'I voted yes,' he smiles. 'But can't you take sick leave, the day after the revolution?'

'Herr Doktor' – I try to make my point, coughing – 'I fear there is no such thing as the day after the revolution.'

'True.' Herr Doktor smiles, then gets serious. 'But listen: cough linctus only suppresses the symptoms. It doesn't deal with the cause. Go and do your thing now, and do it as well as you can. But next week, when the media moves on to another topic, you switch off the phone and listen to what your body is telling you. Otherwise it'll only be a matter of time before your system collapses.'

2

While Deutsche Wohnen & Co. enteignen was pursuing its *radically legal* project of housing socialisation, a Berliner judge, Birgit Malsack-Winkemann, was fantasising about storming the Reichstag. Judge Malsack-Winkemann was not a mere daydreamer. In August 2021, she toured the Reichstag with two ex-soldiers of the Special Forces Command, who could approach the matter strategically. As a former MP of the far-right populist party Alternative for Germany (AfD), Judge Malsack-Winkemann was permitted to enter the Reichstag at any time, with guests. She later testified that her commando friends were only visiting as tourists. And, as tourists do, they took a lot of photos – of the entrances to the Reichstag, the emergency exits, corridors, stairwells, the underground garage and the passage to the nearest metro station.

Judge Malsack-Winkemann's main partner in crime was Heinrich XIII Prince Reuss. This 71-year-old real-estate broker is very attached to his royal title – even though royal privileges were abolished in Germany in 1919. Before that, the Reuss family ruled a small state in what is now Thuringia. In a 2019 lecture at the WorldWebForum in Zurich, Heinrich XIII was strongly critical of modern democracy. Until the abolition of the aristocracy, he argued, 'people were leading happy lives', under a system that was fair for everyone – whereas now 'the tax rates ... force you to work until September, October of each year'. He seems concerned about a failure of political representation: 'If something was not going well, you approached the prince. Who are you supposed to turn [to] today? To your parliamentarian – local, federal, or EU level? Good luck!'[1]

Heinrich XIII and Judge Malsack-Winkemann were part of the *Reichsbürger* [Citizens of the Reich] movement. This revisionist group asserts that the German Reich still exists within its pre-Second World War borders, which extended well into modern-day Poland. They do not consider the Federal Republic of Germany a legitimate state, but 'a limited liability company' – a profit-driven enterprise imposed on the German Reich by the Allies. If the *Reichsbürger* were successful in storming the Reichstag, they would dissolve the Federal Republic of Germany and 'reactivate' the Reich.

In this new-old German Reich, Prince Reuss planned to install himself as head of state. The ministry of justice was reserved for Birgit Malsack-Winkemann. When she became a judge in Berlin's regional court, she must have sworn to uphold the *Grundgesetz*. But you can't make an omelette without breaking eggs, and so Judge Malsack-Winkemann had decided that, in order to make Germany 'sovereign and just' again, the *Grundgesetz* had to be overthrown.

On 7 December 2022, German federal police arrested Birgit Malsack-Winkemann and Heinrich Reuss, along with twenty-three other people, and charged them with planning a coup. It was the biggest police raid in the history of the Federal Republic. The officers stormed over 150 locations, securing 382 firearms, 50 kilograms of gold and €420,000 in cash. The paper trail suggests that a significant quantity of weapons still remains hidden in unidentified locations. In December 2023, the federal prosecutor charged sixty-nine people with terrorism. The suspects include businessmen, lawyers, a retired paratrooper, a tenor, a top chef – and a fortune teller, whom Judge Malsack-Winkemann had hired, on a public salary, as her assistant in the Bundestag. The fortune teller didn't see the police raid coming.

The liberal public likes to laugh at the *Reichsbürger*, as it does at Donald Trump, Jarosław Kaczyński and even Vladimir Putin. The liberal public also likes to laugh at their supporters. They are often dismissed as *irrational*, implying greater rationality on the part of whoever is criticising them. This laughter makes the liberal public feel better about themselves – until, one day, the liberal public realises that the 'liberal democratic basic order', as the *Grundgesetz* calls it, is about to be dismantled.

As I write these paragraphs, in January 2024, political analysts are predicting that the AfD – the far-right anti-immigrant party of which Judge Malsack-Winkemann was a member – is currently polling around 32 per cent in the run-up to this year's local elections in the federal states of Brandenburg, Saxony and Thuringia. If these predictions prove true, it might be impossible to form a government without them.

The AfD was launched in 2013 by a group of academic economists in reaction to a European crisis: they were opposed to Germany financing the bailouts of poorer southern European countries. Soon afterwards – and not without some internal party struggles – the AfD switched strategy: it started fuelling populist anger, directing it at refugees and migrants in particular.

The AfD's usual argument goes like this: how come the government is spending money on foreigners when Frau Müller – an honest German woman who worked hard as a nurse her entire life – can barely afford to pay her rent?

Frau Müller is not a rhetorical example. She is my friend's neighbour, a real person. She votes for the AfD.

Of course, Frau Müller's Syrian neighbour is not the real source of her problems. But launching into a passionate polemic with Frau Müller is unlikely to work, because it fails to address the most important point, which is: this argument only ever works if the *emotional* aspect is real. Frau Müller *really was* overwhelmed with fear when she first read a letter about the rent increase. And she *really was* angry. 'Is it fair,' she asked my friend, who had criticised her political choice, 'that, after a lifetime of work those people [i.e. the government] had the nerve to call "essential", I'm afraid I'll lose my home in my retirement?'

People's anger always *starts* with something real: a loss they have suffered, or an unmet need. If the loss is processed, if the need is met in time, the anger abates of its own accord. But if people's losses are not properly acknowledged, if their needs remain unmet for a long time, the anger grows. Once it passes a certain threshold, the anger becomes detached from its original cause, and righteous anger transforms into 'free-floating rage'.[2]

Free-floating rage is diffuse, boundless, and available for cynical appropriation and manipulation. This is because rage is painful. It creates tension in the body that has to be released, because otherwise it becomes unbearable for the person experiencing it. The easiest way to release the tension of rage is to externalise it, by projecting it onto someone or something else. This is why people in a rage are often violent. Another way to alleviate rage is for people to feel they are seen and embraced by a community. No matter what the cause, anger is born of perceived injustice. It turns into free-floating rage only when the original injustice is not repaired, or at least properly acknowledged by others.

Rage escalates from a sense that one's suffering is not being taken seriously. Because humans are neurobiologically wired for connection, a sense of community is far more important for healing anger than analytical accuracy in naming its causes. In any case, these causes might be unclear from the start. Anger does not arise in the body with a ready-made explanation of where it has come from. It takes emotional work to fully understand the sources of one's own anger. Because a raging person seeks an immediate release of tension, a semblance of analysis is usually good enough – as long as it comes with an acknowledgement of the suffering, or a promise of relief.[3]

While the psychology of rage-driven populism has been long understood, social scientists have sought to explain the geographical patterns of the AfD's success. Its leadership is predominantly West German, but the AfD has been most overwhelmingly popular in the former East. *Reichsbürger* are also a predomin-antly East German phenomenon. This suggests that populist leaders are tapping into a larger reserve of free-floating rage that exists in these regions in particular. What are the origins of such rage?

We will never have analytical certainty about this. Because free-floating rage is detached from its original causes, we cannot depend on raging voters to give a credible account of its sources. However, research suggests that one important trigger may be the East German version of economic 'shock therapy'. The *Treuhandanstalt* in particular – a Western-led, top-down privatisa-tion agency – has been recognised as an 'emotional bad bank' in the former East. The mere mention of the *Treuhandanstalt* pro-vokes 'strong emotional and outstandingly negative reactions'. Easterners' anger about privatisation is still present, 'like a smoldering fire beneath the surface'.[4]

But East Germany does not have the monopoly on social anger. 'The AfD is no longer an eastern phenomenon, but has become a major all-German party. So we have arrived.' These were the words of Alice Weidel, the AfD's coleader, celebrating the election results in the state of Hesse in 2023. The AfD came second, securing 18.4 per cent of the vote. Hesse is a West German powerhouse state that includes Frankfurt, the financial hub of Europe. Alice Weidel has a PhD in international develop-ment. She previously worked for Goldman Sachs and the Bank of China. It's much harder to laugh at Alice Weidel, or dismiss her as *irrational*. She looks like she knows exactly what she's doing.

3

When Poland's 'Law and Justice' (*Prawo i Sprawiedliwość*, PiS) gov-ernment first started dismantling the Constitutional Tribunal in 2015, the international media published photos of public protests in Warsaw. The tiny dot of my head must be somewhere in those photos. The liberal Polish press, however, decried the fact that, in a country of 40 million, only a few thousand educated, middle-class people rallied to condemn the political attack on the rule of law. I was not surprised. Around that time, I was writing up my analysis of the 'Reprivatisationgate' scandal I described earlier in this book. I had spoken to many tenants who had lost their homes to fraudulent businessmen in judicial proceedings that were portrayed to the public as 'historical justice'. These former tenants did not regard the judicial system as a neutral dispenser of justice.

Many of those people supported PiS – in part because PiS politicians were among the first to publicly address the injustice of reprivatisation. Back then, the PiS was an opposition party, so to some extent this might have been a purely tactical move. However, the 'Law and Justice Party', in accordance with its name, has long campaigned on a promise to renew the rule of law, which appeared to have been broken by the behind-closed-doors politics of liberal judges. For the PiS, 'Reprivatisationgate' offered proof that the rule of law had never been apolitical: the party used it as an excuse to impose its own politics on the rule of law and disregard all democratic procedures.

Both Poland's two largest parties, the PO (Civic Platform) and the PiS, are the products of an internal split in Solidarność. The Civic Platform consists of liberals who first endorsed the shock therapy, then consistently denied its downsides. In its early years, the PiS spelled out what liberals knew but feared to admit: that, for the majority of the population, shock therapy failed to deliver much of what was promised – and often caused a palpable loss in social and economic status. In more recent years, the PiS has mostly switched to fuelling populist rage with anti-immigrant and anti-European sentiments.

According to the sociologist David Ost, the steep rise of right-wing populism in Poland can be traced back to long-dismissed anger at the economic injustice of the shock therapy. I never voted for the PiS, but I, too, am angry at politicians who continue to deny the impoverishment and dispossession that the shock therapy unleashed in my city, and which also caused my family to suffer.

Solidarność was launched as a democratic movement when the workers from the Gdańsk shipyard responded with solidarity to the anger of the tram driver Henryka Krzywonos. And it collapsed as a democratic movement when its representatives refused to acknowledge the legitimate reasons for people's anger. Few politicians had the courage to admit that they were ashamed they had abandoned solidarity as a core value of the movement. Jacek Kuroń was a prominent exception. Many others covered up their abandonment of solidarity with a superficial appeal to other important values – notably: freedom and the rule of law.

Today, whenever the liberal public deploy the ideas of freedom and the rule of law to shame the raging masses, I cannot help but think that *they do not do the rule of law justice*. People's belief in the justice of the rule of law can only be sustained if they trust that they will be treated like its supposed protagonists: as free, equal and dignified subjects.

Why has the rule of law become so fragile? I don't think that the rule of law has *become* fragile. I think the rule of law has *always* been fragile. This fragility comes from its foundational paradox, which binds together law and politics. It's a marvellous paradox; scholars are constantly unpeeling new layers of it. It concerns legitimation.

According to systems theory, this paradox is in fact a structural coupling of two paradoxes. Firstly: law operates according to a binary code of legal/illegal, yet law cannot legitimise itself simply by declaring itself legal. Unlike the fabled Baron Munchhausen, we cannot pull ourselves out of a mire by our own hair. Politics finds itself in a similar predicament. If the sovereign – whether a king or a people – truly is sovereign, what forces them to observe their own rules? To save each other from these crises of legitimation, law and politics externalise their paradoxes and project them onto each other. The result is state constitution: politics legitimates law, while law legitimates politics.[5]

Because of its paradoxical origins, the rule of law holds different, conflicting truths together. The first contradiction of law relates to violence. Law is the opposite of violence, because it replaces the 'wild' and potentially endless violence of retribution with a rules-based order.[6] Yet law can only do this by becoming, in the words of Walter Benjamin, the ultimate 'mythical' violence.[7] When a judge interpreted the law in a way that allowed me to stay in my apartment, my landlord experienced it as violence – because he knew that the state had the tools to force him to comply. When a tenant is legally evicted because they cannot afford the rent, she experiences it as violence. In the everyday, peaceful operations of the law, violence is always present, if only as a threat.

The second contradiction in the rule of law concerns its supposed neutrality. Legal interpretation, although bound by internal rules, can never fully escape politics. If there were a single, 'objective' way of interpreting the law, there would be no legal disputes. Ultimately, 'any version of what it means for courts to be non-political must come from politics'.[8]

The third contradiction in the rule of law derives from the legal fiction of the 'free and equal subject'. This fiction masks material inequalities, between capital and labour, for example, thereby structurally entangling law with capitalism.[9] However, because maintaining this fiction is necessary for the law to legitimise itself, law also becomes a tool of social emancipation. This is why E. P. Thomson (not uncontroversially) called the rule of law 'an unqualified, universal good'.[10]

What makes the rule of law universal is indeed its paradoxical nature. A paradox is a tension field within which it becomes possible to transgress the limitations of each opposing pole. Yet the tension of holding conflicting truths together can become explosive if an equitable balance is not maintained. This is why, throughout history, the rule of law has repeatedly fallen into crisis. These crises are genuinely dangerous. What is at stake in them is not even the rule of law – which persists in some form even under authoritarianism – but something more delicate and important. It is something indispensable that, according to the legal sociologist Gunther Teubner, 'legal sociology has no idea of' – justice.[11]

Nothing can guarantee that the rule of law will provide justice. Justice is 'the legal system's *memento mori*, a reminder of its own limitations'.[12] And because society is a dynamic process, there will never be an ultimate definition of justice. Yet if a political community doesn't *feel* that the legal system *works towards* justice, the rule of law loses its legitimacy.

4

When I tell the journalist Herr Steiner that the rule of law is undergoing a 'midlife crisis', it is, of course, a metaphor. But I find this metaphor *clinically* useful.[13] Because the rule of law is similar to the way Jungian psychology describes human nature: a paradoxical whole driven by opposing tendencies. And while the rule of law is not a person, capable of transforming themselves to escape from crisis, the people who uphold it – lawyers, politicians and us, members of the democratic society – are just that: people.

According to Jung, a midlife crisis results from the excess tension that arises from suppressing some of our qualities into our 'shadow' in order to preserve our 'persona', an ego-ideal that we choose to display in public. But the more we repress something, the greater the power with which it strikes back. The force of repression distorts the original content. Ultimately, what bites us back is a monstrous version of everything we had hoped to get rid of.

The ego-ideal of liberal democracy is 'a government of laws, not men': a sealed-off system immune to external influences and maintained by neutral experts. Of course, no one really believes in that; people do not *experience* the rule of law this way. But governments and jurists often (and usually for *political* reasons) become overly invested in maintaining the image of law as wholly apolitical. The politics inherent in the law – the spirit of written laws, the uneven power relations within a political system, the room for legal interpretation – is suppressed into the rule of law's dark shadow. Sooner or later, politics strikes back at the law in monstrous form: the 'Law and Justice' party dismantles the Constitutional Tribunal, and a judge makes plans to storm the Reichstag.

The paradoxical nature of the rule of law is not a 'problem' that we can 'solve'. It is a tension field that we need to manage.

Jung calls the management of this tension field 'shadow-work', because it assumes that we are letting the shadow in, and learning to narrate and manage it as an official part of who we are. In doing that, shadow-work reduces the tension of suppression. This allows us consciously (or, within a political community, democratically) to negotiate the terms on which the shadow inhabits the system. Such transparent, public negotiations of the terms on which politics inhabits the law are, in my opinion, one of the most important features of the political strategy of Deutsche Wohnen & Co. enteignen.

As a Berliner, I support DWE's project of socialising housing. As a scholar-activist, I have written this book with a much broader purpose: I want to postulate *radically legal politics* as a path for deepening our democracies and renewing the rule of law. I believe that this type of democratic engagement with the law – prototyped by DWE – could effectively protect the structural fragility of the rule of law from being exploited by authoritarian populism.

DWE's *radically legal politics* is premised on shadow-work being done on two levels: emotional shadow-work performed within the political system; and political shadow-work within the legal system.

The first level of shadow-work embraces the emotions of a population affected by a systemic injustice – like the fear and anger of tenants affected by the housing crisis. These emotions are usually suppressed by the mainstream political parties, and often don't appear in the political sphere until much too late, after the original anger has transformed into free-floating rage and can no longer be grasped analytically – yet is ripe for manipulation.

Using the techniques of community organising, DWE works to embrace the tenants' anger directly, at its original source. Yet even when confronted with misdirected rage – during door-to-door campaigning, for example – DWE's activists do not engage in political polemics, or dismiss their interlocutor's worldview. This is considered disrespectful, and lacking in curiosity as to how people have arrived at their set of convictions. The purpose of DWE's campaigning is much humbler: it aims to trace the element of anger related to housing injustice back to its root cause.

When DWE works with people to diagnose the roots of their anger, the diagnosis is specific, preceded by analysis. The reason for Frau Müller's anger – and for her rent increase – is not narrated as a conspiracy of 'corrupt elites', or even as a large and abstract cause such as 'capitalism': rather, it is the subsumption of specific parts of the housing sector under the profit-driven logic of the financial sector. In the process, people's raw anger can be transformed into what Martha Nussbaum calls 'Transition-Anger' – a constructive anger aimed at improving overall social welfare, rather than at retribution. DWE's vision of a new housing system proves Nussbaum's point that Transition-Anger is 'very important in thinking about political institutions'.

Parallel to the emotional shadow-work that deals with anger, DWE also does the shadow-work within the rule of law – by finding and publicly narrating the *political* opportunities offered by the legal system. A political cause of alleviating a systemic injustice is therefore provided with a precise and achievable legal solution. DWE found such a solution in Article 15, and followed up with a proposition for embedding this solution into the existing system.

On the political ground, the law lends the cause systemic credibility, and directs energy from general deliberations towards very concrete tasks on which the legal process is premised. This legal credibility has an emotional effect – people *feel* that the injustice they have suffered is being taken seriously, by the legal system as well. The sense of community created through organising transforms anger into joy, and redirects the need for agency from retribution to constituting the future. And ultimately this sense of agency spreads from the activists to the general population, as people can finally *do* something (add their signature, vote, put up a poster) with a credible expectation that it will impact the system.

When the legal argument works politically in the public sphere, the two types of shadow-work reinforce each other like interlocking cogs: the emotional energy fuels the legal work, and the legal work fuels the enthusiasm. Consequently, *radically legal politics* can be impressively effective. It is also very demanding, as it relies on many different skills: working with emotions, organising a political campaign, legal engineering, and building relationships within the broader political system. Radically legal politics is therefore premised on the internal diversity of the group: it is *radically democratic*.

5

What does it mean to be *radically democratic*? To me, it means the willingness to work with people we otherwise disagree with – and to use our differences as a resource for learning, rather than as a pretext to destroy one another. But liberal democracy has an ego ideal too. Regardless of whether we call it a 'melting pot' or a 'tossed salad', it assumes that our differences will be consumable and easy to digest. In reality, negotiating those differences – and our freedoms – usually entails both wins and losses.

Democracy is not the peaceful coexistence of multitudes. In the best case scenario, it is a well-managed conflict. The same is true of a democratic movement. Any diverse group is a social forcefield in which all the problems of wider society will eventually resurface. The success of a democratic movement is therefore equally dependent on its political or legal strategy and on its capacity to manage internal conflicts. This is not easy: activists are people too, and each carries their individual shadow.

DWE came closest to an internal split in the summer of 2021, when – just as we had secured all the signatures needed for the referendum – a female activist reported an incident of sexual harassment by an older male activist. As so often in cases like these, with no witnesses, there was no way to prove or disprove either the claim or the rebuttal. In the midst of an already demanding campaign, the movement was thrown headfirst into all the emotional complexity of #MeToo.

We weren't prepared for this. The law couldn't help: the gulf between the legalistic unprovability of such cases and their sociological prevalence is at the heart of the ongoing public controversy. There were no pre-agreed procedures, and no course of action would be neutral. Some people took upon themselves the authority to act quickly. Others resented their actions. The conflict quickly spilled over from the affected parties to the whole DWE body, manifesting especially strongly across generational divides. For some, the situation reactivated memories of past trauma. Others felt they were suffering new and unmerited injustices in the present. People's intense emotional reactions reduced their capacity to express their positions empathetically.

To alleviate the emotional after-effects of the conflict, DWE's Coordination Circle authorised R. and me to organise two sessions of conflict mediation with external facilitators. By then, both parties involved had left the movement: the meetings were intended for anyone else who felt emotionally affected. About forty people attended the meetings. It is hard objectively to assess their impact: I can only legitimately speak of how these meetings affected my own perceptions of the conflict.

The facilitators' interventions helped me to see how our opposing positions all upheld values that were important for the whole group, such as empathy, or lawfulness. Also, it was a relief to be able to express suppressed emotions, or even to see them escalate in a safe environment. None of this made conflicted people suddenly agree with one another – but in some cases it did enable them to *see* one another. Of course, two meetings alone are not going to work magic. Some people still decided to leave the movement in the aftermath, which I consider a loss. Overall, though, as a movement, we have survived – and we have learnt from it.

As the movement grows and develops, DWE activists are learning on the job how to manage different kinds of tension that are also present in general society. Often, it is hard to differentiate between the overlapping sources of these conflicts: concrete situations always exist within a social context, and empathy often competes with exhaustion.

T. recalls a situation when he was already suffering from severe burnout, having been working very long hours for the movement in several capacities. T. is male, non-German and a member of the Right to the City working group. He and others put a great deal of effort into designing procedures that would actively include people marginalised by a lack of German language skills and/or citizenship. When B., a German activist of Turkish origin, referred to the Right to the City working group as a bunch of white migrants who weren't serious about their activism, T. felt that she had dismissed the group's efforts without knowing much about it. He flew into rage.

As the incident unfolded, other activists present made an effort to work through the tension of the conflict together. C. spoke empathetically about everyone's nerves being frayed from the pre-referendum stress. Over the days that followed, she took action to mediate the conflict. F. called T. the next day to discuss the situation and how to fix it. T. welcomed this intervention, but he tells me that he is still resentful, and feels his objections to B.'s statement were not taken seriously enough. Nonetheless, he remains a committed member of DWE. He says he is gradually learning to manage his workload to forestall another burnout.

A. recalls how strongly she felt about the conflict over the collection of signatures. DWE agreed that, in order to make a political statement, we would also collect the (legally invalid) signatures of non-German Berliners. The question was whether to collect them on the same list or a separate one. A., like many other migrants, was invested in the idea of a separate list. But, after a long and heated discussion, the general assembly decided otherwise. 'I think that what I've learnt in DWE,' A. tells me, 'is to lose with grace. To lose and still keep going.'

This ability – to lose with grace and still keep going, without wanting to destroy one's opponent – is demonstrably lacking in contemporary politics. Ultimately, it allowed DWE to maintain its energy after the government deliberately ignored the results of the first referendum. We are angry about this. But we have channelled this anger into writing a law for the second referendum. We are not storming the Reichstag.

Because I say 'we' are angry – and because I am a scholar-activist – you might wonder whether I am neutral in my research.

Let me assure you that I am not. I care about democracy and the ability of humans to thrive. This has never been a neutral position. But mainstream academia still preserves an ego-ideal of the hyperrational scientist, devoid of values and feelings. Yet this ideal has long since been scientifically disproved.

Research in neuroscience shows that no rationality is possible without feelings. Patients with damage to brain areas responsible for processing emotions are unable to take even simple decisions – even though their intelligence remains intact. If they have to choose between different options, they can correctly describe the factual differences between those options, but they lack the capacity to evaluate them. For patients like these, even choosing what to eat for lunch is a struggle. A difference only makes a difference if you can *feel* it.

Emotions are an integral part of our rationality. They serve as rapid processing systems to evaluate options and help us arrive at decisions. Just as thoughts appear in the head, feelings manifest themselves in the body to provide us with crucial information. And just like thoughts, emotions are not always correct or adequate to cope with the situation.

The methodology of social sciences has long relied on the skill of critical thinking: the ability to discern information and weigh evidence, while also establishing distance from one's own assumptions in order to consider different perspectives. The neuroscientist Rolf Reber postulates that this skillset should be complemented with 'critical feeling'. A critical feeler uses emotions as a source of information – but is also able to see their own emotions from a critical distance, assess reasons behind their own emotional responses and gather information to check whether they are adequate to the situation. Once we gather new information, our feelings – just like thoughts – often adapt to the new knowledge.[14]

We cannot escape from feelings – all we can do is think critically about their sources. In a similar vein, we often *feel* that a statement is not right well before we can analytically grasp why. By narrating my personal engagement openly, I hope to provide you with more data rather than less, namely: what

I have found out through my research, but also why and how I have been seeking answers.

As a scholarly narrator, I don't want to pretend any longer that I am omniscient and neutral. I would rather be critical and tender.[15] And I believe that constantly moving between theory and practice has made me a better scholar. In the words of Kurt Lewin, who first coined the term 'action research': 'You cannot understand the system until you try to change it.'[16]

6

Sometimes, trying both to change the system and to understand it puts me in a contradictory position. One of the aspects of research I most enjoy is exploring such contradictions and using them as opportunities for learning. This was why I invited Peter Kadas, a global financier and the sponsor of the Nine Dots Prize, to a High Table dinner at King's College, Cambridge. As I donned my black academic gown – the obligatory apparel for such dinners – I really felt like Batwoman about to enter Gotham.

If I make a checklist of all the things I have ever criticised in my research, Peter has done them all. Firstly, he built his fortune on privatising eastern Europe. Born and raised in socialist Hungary, he defected to Canada in the 1980s, where he got a business degree. Because of his familiarity with both the context and the language, in 1990, an investment bank sent him back to eastern Europe and tasked him with 'figuring things out'. By figuring it out, Peter became very successful. 'You remember the Polish chocolate you ate as a child?' he asks me, at pre-dinner drinks. 'We privatised it!'

Two decades later – around the time I was facing my landlord in court – Peter acquired 'a portfolio of 10,000 apartments' in Berlin. A fund co-founded by Peter only saw one of these apartments, and he can't quite remember where they were located ('mostly East Berlin, I think'). In the summer of 2011, the fund lost the apartments to the bank. He is no longer sure quite what happened, but he remembers it as the apartments being 'effectively stolen' from him. Probably – Peter winks at me – it had something to do with some tenancy regulations. But wait – let's savour the appetizers before rushing straight to the dessert.

Meeting on the foreign territory of British politeness, Peter and I instantly connect through our homespun eastern European humour. Our obvious conflict of interest becomes a whetstone on which to sharpen our wits. And so, having passed the butter to the biologist on my left, we go on to dissect the elephant right there on High Table. We agree that, on some higher spiritual plane, karma has given us what we wanted. Peter conceived the Nine Dots Prize to promote ideas that, because they are innovative, might seem controversial – so he can't complain if my idea is controversial *to him*. For my part, the publishing contract gives me total freedom in how I choose to write this book. This is the kind of freedom I crave: it allows me to write about my research without using academic jargon – a powerful reader repellent.

As the Polish (of course she is!) waitress serves us the main course, I enquire further about Peter's Berlin apartments. Since he can't remember all the details, he promises to connect me with his colleagues in Canada. And a week later, I hear the familiar story told from the other side of the looking-glass. Characteristically, they rarely use the word 'apartments'; it's either 'the assets' or simply 'the portfolio'.

The portfolio, which I receive as an Excel spreadsheet, is a smorgasbord of 12,781 properties. Looking through the list, I get a sense of how hard it is, at this volume, to remember what one 'owns' (and of course Peter never owned these apartments directly, as a person, they were owned by the fund). In fact, 'only' 3,673 apartments from Peter's portfolio were in Berlin – but this would still qualify for DWE's socialisation plan (my turn to wink!). Contrary to what Peter recalled, the Berlin apartments were not prefab blocks in the former East. These 'assets' were mostly early twentieth-century high-ceilinged tenements, and were scattered all across the city. The rest of the portfolio was in North Rhine-Westphalia, with two commercial properties in Poland thrown into the mix.

How did Peter 'lose' his Berlin apartments? His colleague, who referred to it as 'the accident', guided me through what happened. But wait – the cheese platter has just arrived at High Table. For discretion, in describing 'the accident', I'll replace companies' names with cheeses.

In early 2010, Camembert – one of the fund's many companies – bought Danablu, an indebted company listed in Denmark. Danablu owned the portfolio (the apartments in Berlin and elsewhere) through Limburger, a German limited liability company. In order to buy Limburger, Danablu had borrowed several chunks of money (financial tranches) from various German and Danish lenders. When buying Danablu, Camembert switched the loans from variable interest rates to fixed ones using a financial tool called swaps. By swapping the variable rates for fixed ones, Danablu ensured that the interest rates on Limburger's loans would remain steady and predictable, making it easier for them to calculate future expenses. However, as a result of the change, the loans appeared to have lost value, because market interest rates were very low at the time.

According to Peter's colleague, the essence of 'the accident' was this. In 2011, Berlin Hyp – one of the German lenders – terminated the swap agreement without communicating properly with Danablu. A big lump sum payment fell due. Danablu couldn't pay this unexpected bill, so one chunk of the loan went into default. Because these chunks of money (financial tranches) were interconnected, the problem spread to two others, meaning that these were now also due for repayment. Danablu was forced to declare bankruptcy for all the financial tranches affected. In other words: the handling of the loans by Berlin Hyp meant Limburger turned into a stinking deal.

Peter's business lost €15 million in equity as a result of 'the accident'. When I ask his colleague if this is unusual, he describes it as 'annoying', but also 'part of the risk in acquiring highly leveraged companies with the expectation of making an outsized return in a market that was pretty dislocated at the time'.[17] Fair enough. In any case, their bankruptcy had nothing to do with housing regulations, only with how the financial institutions acted, or, as Peter's colleague put it, 'the incompetence and over-confidence of the bank'. (As a researcher, I must point out that this is a one-sided account: Berlin Hyp would presumably see it differently.) Finally, I ask what impact this loss had on Peter's overall business position. 'No impact,' his colleague replies.

Laughing with Peter across High Table, I certainly get the impression that, having lost 3,673 Berlin apartments, he recovered better than most people who only lose one. And, as I laugh, I suddenly remember what DWE's conflict facilitators taught us: that laughter, even genuine, often serves as a psychological coping mechanism to release the tension of an underlying conflict. Certainly, thinking back to when I couldn't afford to rent an apartment in Warsaw, I laugh less.

By the end of our conversation, Peter is willing to make some concessions. 'I will give it to you,' he says, 'that finance's impact on housing has got a bit out of control. Not even successful professionals can afford to buy an apartment any more!' However, he still thinks socialisation would set a dangerous precedent: 'If we socialise apartments today, wouldn't people want to socialise shoe factories tomorrow?'

Benedicto benedicatur: Let a blessing be given by the blessed one. The Provost of King's College brings the dinner to a close with the customary grace, and Peter and I agree to continue our discussion next time. As I walk him to his taxi, Peter issues a final threat: he might buy up the entire print run of this book to stop my ideas from spreading. I smile back and say nothing; I wouldn't want to spoil such a friendly joke. This book is under a Creative Commons license. It is available to everyone, for free.

7

This book is like one of those modern theatre plays: the public will decide how the story ends (Figure 6.1). I close my laptop. I water the plants in my Berlin home. I look at the clock: I have to leave soon. At the last full stop of this story, the story will pick me up and carry me on.

As I leave my study, I pause for a moment in the hallway of my apartment. Rain was pouring from the skies of Berlin when

I first came here in 2007 – and as I entered, I immediately felt at home. But it wasn't yet my home, back then; I was only there for an interview. Max, Thorsten and Carla explained to me this was neither a 'cuddly flat-share' like the one on the *Friends* TV show, nor an unsociable apartment-sharing arrangement just to split the rent. 'We eat some meals together, and we respect each other's freedom,' said Max.

The next day, Max called me to say that they had chosen someone else. They liked me, he said, but there had been so many likeable candidates. I said I understood, and slowly sank into a puddle of sadness. But Max didn't hang up. I started to feel irritated that, after this news, he still expected me to go on making small talk. A full five minutes later, he told me he had been joking. I had got the room – and thereafter became a regular victim of Max's practical jokes.

I peek into the room I first moved into. It's now my daughter's room. A brass hook shaped like a horse is still on the inside of the door. It belonged to one of the many roommates who lived here before me. Wondering if the horse was Regina's, or maybe Annika's, I enter the living room. This used to be Lisa's room – and it was me who got to choose Lisa as a flatmate. But I wasn't cool enough to play Max's joke on her: I liked her so much that I invited her to move in straight away.

In Lisa's room, we spent long hours discussing legal strategies. This was in 2012, when Herr Meier first wanted us out. Housing prices were already rising in Berlin, but tenant protection laws make it difficult to raise the rent within an existing contract. Herr Meier knew that if he got rid of us, he could charge more.

The original rental contract was signed in 1999 by four German students, who were all given the status of a contract party (*Hauptmieter*). Each time someone moved out, the new flatmate had to go to Herr Becker – Herr Meier's building manager – to sign an appendix to the original contract. My appendix states that I was entering into the contract in place of Regina.

Each time there was an exchange of flatmates, Herr Becker made tea and asked us about the condition of the apartment.

When Max moved out, Herr Becker allocated some money for sanding the floorboards in his room (it was high time, he suggested). Herr Becker always asked the new tenants what music they liked. He had grown up in East Germany, and would often talk about his favourite concerts at the Leipzig Opera.

Just before Lisa moved in, Herr Meier fired Herr Becker. He then refused to prepare the usual appendix, or add Lisa to the contract. It was clear that he hoped to dissolve our flatshare. A colleague from university advised me to join a tenants' union. I did, and together with Lisa we attended free consultations with several of the union's lawyers. They all came up with similar diagnoses of our problem, but they each proposed a slightly different solution. It was clear that, written laws notwithstanding, our future depended on their legal interpretation.

I still live here. Evidently, the law has protected me well enough. But like many real-life victories, mine was preceded by some serious losses. When Lisa and I first explained our case to the lawyers, they all agreed that it was a legal grey zone. On the one hand, there was no written law that protected tenant exchange within a multi-party tenancy agreement. On the other, this was very typical practice with Berlin flatshares. And, unlike many others, we had a well-preserved paper trail of more than twenty tenant-exchange appendices.

Our case could set a precedent. Herr Wolf, a lawyer-activist, was genuinely excited. In the folder with our appendices – greasy from being stored in the communal kitchen – he saw legal gold. But there was a catch: Herr Meier had refused to add Lisa to the tenancy agreement *before* I joined the tenants' union, so their insurance didn't cover it.

'If we win' – Herr Wolf laid out the options for us – 'Herr Meier will have to pay all your legal fees, and you may end up contributing to the future security of all Berlin flatshares. But if we lose,' he continued, 'there will probably be a sizeable bill. You would then need to cover all the costs, including those of Herr Meier's lawyer.' The risk was on us.

We didn't go for it. With no legal insurance and no back-up money, we feared being saddled with huge debts. We didn't take

Herr Meier to court; we negotiated with him informally instead. As a result, in early 2013, my two existing roommates and I signed a completely new rental contract with our landlord. This new contract stipulated higher rent, which would be indexed every two years to inflation (this was not the case before). It did not include Lisa as a contract party, and foreclosed the path to any future exchange of tenants within the contract.

The terms of the new contract were significantly worse than those of the original one. Why did we sign it? Legally speaking, we signed it *freely*. From the lawyers we consulted, I knew that Herr Meier had no legal way of forcing us to terminate the old contract. But we still needed a new flatmate, and I had already promised Lisa that she could move in. Without taking him to court, we could not force Herr Meier to add Lisa to the old contract. What we ended up doing – signing a separate sublet contract with Lisa, with Herr Meier's agreement – was our legal right.

Herr Meier had initially denied us this right. A sublet requires the owner's agreement. This is usually just a formality; the owner must give serious and specific legal reasons for denying it. Herr Meier had no valid reasons – but to prove it, we would have to go to court. In this case, losing was not a serious risk: the right to sublet has a solid basis in written laws *and* well-established precedents. Practically, though, it would mean that Lisa could not move in until the court case was over. It would probably take a year. By then, it wasn't just a question of sharing costs – Lisa had become my best friend.

A year later, she got a scholarship at the University of Frankfurt. When Lisa moved out, Herr Meier again refused to let the new flatmate move in. He also tried to increase the rent, in several different ways. Now, though, we were covered by the legal insurance. Four times I took Herr Meier to court to enforce the rights afforded to me by written laws – and I was only able to do it thanks to the support of the tenant union. Each time, I won.

Meanwhile, Herr Wolf has won a precedent-setting case almost identical to ours – Lisa and I read about it at breakfast one morning, in the tenant union's bulletin. So we could have won. But that's the nature of risk: you might also lose. The new contract indexes my rent to inflation, and in the last few years especially, there has been a sharp increase. I don't pay one of those mythically cheap old Berlin rents, or a crazily expensive one, like those demanded in Prenzlauer Berg today. On the Berlin spectrum, I sit in the middle that, for now, appears to be safe.

Oh dear, I shall be late! I have to make it to DWE's special plenary. Today we're discussing our procedure for working with the law firm that's drafting the socialisation law for the second referendum. As I pass the kitchen, I grab the half-eaten Berliner Mira has left on the table. I run down the stairs to the tram stop. The tram is late; it should be here already. This is annoying, but not unusual. Ultimately, it always comes.

Figure 7.1 Dancing before the law
(*Source:* Ian Clotworthy/DWE)

Before the law, there stands a guard.
Franz Kafka, writer and lawyer, Berliner in the
years 1923–24

It's all about the right mix – even if it means letting in the odd lawyer in a double-breasted suit with his Gucci-Prada wife.
Sven Marquardt, the bouncer at Berghain, Berlin's
legendary techno club

BEFORE THE LAW

Franz Kafka feat. DWE

Before the law, there stands a guard.[1] We arrive in front of him, a small group from the big city. We seek admittance to the law. But the guard says he cannot admit us just now.

'We can come again,' we say. 'When is it possible to enter?'

'It might be possible to enter, but not now. And not later. Come earlier,' he snickers, 'years earlier than now. Then it might be possible.'

But the gate to the law stands open, as it always does. When the guard steps aside, we stoop to get a view of the inside. The guard notices us doing this.

'If you're so tempted, why don't you try and get in in spite of me,' he laughs. 'But remember: I am mighty. And I am just the lowest of all the guards. From room to room there are guards, each more powerful than the one before. I cannot endure even one glimpse of the third!'

We know that the law should be accessible to everyone, always. But we anticipated such difficulties. We have lived long enough in the big city; we have seen those mighty guards. We have waited tables at their incessantly growing galas. Some drank whisky on the black rocks while others, dressed all in red, decreed austerity of the imagination.

We look again at the guard in front of us. His suit is made of price tags; his pockets are sewn shut. We have no time to lose. We will not rush. We will not leave now.

The guard points us to a bench where we can sit down beside the door. There we wait, and wait. We wait for days and years. And we wait joyfully.

Before the law, we build a camp. We decorate the law's gates with flags and ribbons, lush yellow and pansy purple. In the evenings, we dance around the fire and sing songs about the Constitution. We write love letters to the law and raise them above the city squares (Figure 7.1).

We count ourselves, as we count on ourselves, as we count on the law. We write our names on countless scraps of paper. Every day, we count them too. By the time the conkers fall and line the city's wide boulevards, we are 1 million.

Journalists arrive to conduct little interrogations, quizzing us about our homes and much else besides. They question the guard about our prospects of admittance. As the guard hesitates, professors arrive from faraway towns. The professors gasp, and grunt, and roar, and whimper. They wipe the sweat off their shiny foreheads. And they say the same thing, again and again. That the law should be accessible to everyone, always.

As we trouble the guard with our endless enquiries, things start to appear in front of the gate. They are gifts, and threats, and pleas, and promises, all wrapped in sheets of shiny language. 'Take it and go,' the guard says. 'The law will never give you anything better.' We take it and stay. 'The only reason we are accepting this,' we say, 'is so you don't think there's something you've failed to do to make us go.'

Over many years, we observe the doorkeeper almost continuously. He curses us, loudly and recklessly in the early years, then later, as he gets old, merely chuntering under his breath. He becomes a little childish. By now he has made friends with the fleas in his fur collar, and he asks the fleas to help him make us go.

Over time, his eyesight begins to fail. He is unsure whether things around him are getting dark, or whether his eyes are deceiving him. B. brings him a folding chair and K. covers him with a warm blanket. M. pours him some hot tea from her thermos, and C. shares their sandwich with him. It is getting late. In the darkness, we all discern a glory that bursts unquenchably from the gates to the law.

The guard has not much longer to live. Before he retires, he assembles all the experiences of many years into one question, which he has never dared to ask us. He beckons us over, unable to haul his creaking body upright.

We bend over to hear him. The difference in our respective heights has shifted a lot to his disadvantage.

'What is it you want to know?' we ask the guard.

'Many people give up on the law,' he says, 'but you are insatiable. How is it that over so many years you kept insisting on being admitted?'

We see that the man is nearing the end of his life. We pull out a dusty volume of the *Grundgesetz* and point to Article 15.

'This door was intended for all of us,' we say, in unison, to reach his failing ears. 'Now we are going to open it!'

Love
and
Gratitude

To every single letter of Deutsche Wohnen & Co. enteignen: For writing a new world by coming repeatedly together.

To Mira: For you, I want to write a new world – and to finally stop writing. *Córuś, kocham Cię.*

To Grażyna Kusiak: For fostering my light and my shadow. *Mamo, dziękuję.*

To Lisa Eberle: For the first decade of our friendship, and all the decades to come. For laying this book out with me on the wall of a home that we fought for together.

To Simon Müller: For your owlish wisdom, outlandish humour and a human heart.

To Karsten Buch: For being a lifebuoy and a real friend. For being real. For being.

To Ralf Hoffrogge: For conducting interviews together, and for your amazing honesty and integrity. I am looking forward to reading your book!

To Ika Haug, Kalle Kunkel and Bella Rogner: For always responding to my last-minute questions.

To Jane Tinkler: For being the Senior Prize Manager worth the title. For being by my side through all the struggles.

To Charlotte Collins: For being the ultimate language wizard – and for the fun of playing with words together.

To Gillian Tett: For supporting me as a scholar, a mother, and a King's Fellow.

To Sharon McCann: For your grace and patience as I was pushing the boundaries of the editorial process.

To Claire Sissen and Gemma Smith: For the magic of turning this book from a Word file into an object!

To Joanna Page: For the dancing conferences we will organise one day!

To Nicky Dawidowski, Judith Weik and Mette Rokus Jamasb from the CRASSH team: For the support with organising the seminars.

To the participants of the *Radically Legal* seminar at CRASSH: For all your comments. Every single one has helped me.

To Amelia Horgan: For jumping on board at the last moment to help.

To Peter Kadas: For your friendly threats and all the
   future discussions.
To Jessica Jackson and James Douglas: Let's make a Riot!
To David Runcimann: For the advice at *Fitzbillies*.
To Simon Goldhill: For the dinner party I will never forget!
To Matthias Bernt: For the East-Berlin friendship that
   runs globally.
To Kaspar Metzkow: For double-checking all the details.
To Gosia Zmysłowska: For visualising the better tomorrow.
To Ian Clotworthy: For your pictures – and for your
   relentless engagement.
To Anna 'Gabi' Gabryjelska and Alex Hirszfeld: For trusting the
   process with me.
To Karim Niangane: For drawing my storms out.
To Surabhi Ranganathan: For the G5, from where it felt easier to
   see myself achieving this.
To Marcin Szala: For typesetting my luck!
To Max Lewandowski: For the Ryanair serendipity and
   caring supplementation.
To Kasia Grunt-Mejer, Jacek Grunt-Mejer, Julian Dworak, Ritu
   Mittal, Artur Burasz and Orlando Sanchez: For hugs and
   support that came at just the right moments.
To Basia Adamczuk: For being my Polish family in Cambridge.
To Chris Wray: For your hospitality at Fool's Valley.
To King's College, Cambridge: For being my intellectual home.
To all the people who danced with me.

Soundtrack

1 **Taking the Tram Home**
   Jungle/Bella Ciao by Daiana Lou (feat. Berlin Street
      Musicians United)
2 **We Are All Staying Put**
   I Wish I Knew How it Would Feel to be Free by Nina Simone
   Transmission by Joy Division
   I am the Law by T-INA Darling
   Waiting Room by Fugazi
3 **Berlin Becomes High-Risk Capital**
   Say Yes by Wax Tailor (feat. ASM)
   Das Gespenst der Enteignung by The Incredible Herrengedeck
   Deutsche Wohnen Enteignen by The Hans
4 **Who Constitutes Power?**
   Das Grundgesetz by Bodo Wartke
   Befragung eines Kriegsdienstverweigerers by Franz
      Josef Degenhardt
   People Have the Power by Patti Smith
5 **Berlin Is the Greatest Extravaganza**
   Wie lieblich sind deine Wohnungen (Psalm 84.1–2,4) by Johannes
      Brahms, Sir Simon Rattle and Berliner Philharmoniker
   Schwarz zu blau by Peter Fox
   Ist mir egal by BVG (feat. Kazim Akboga)[1]
   Zukunft Pink by Peter Fox (feat. Inéz)
6 **The Rule of Law Is Having a Midlife Crisis**
   Law (Earthlings on Fire) by David Bowie
   Strassenbahn des Todes by Element of Crime
   Running Home by Paula i Karol
7 **Before the Law**
   Freedom by The Gulls

Notes

* The names of private people appearing in the book (my landlord, lawyers, state officials) are changed to protect their anonymity.

Chapter 1

1 The UN Research Institute for Social Development proposes the term 'solidarity economy' to describe economic activities oriented towards social sustainability and participatory governance. Cf. Peter Utting, Jean-Louis Laville and United Nations Research Institute for Social Development (eds), *Social and Solidarity Economy: Beyond the Fringe* (London: Zed Books, 2015).

2 Ralf Hoffrogge, 'Nie wirklich weg. Fünf Formen von Gemeineigentum in der Geschichte und ihre Bedeutung für das Ringen um Vergesellschaftung heute' (2024) 1 *Arbeit – Bewegung – Geschichte. Zeitschrift für Historische Studien* 10–33.

Chapter 2

1 Walter Benjamin, 'Critique of Violence', trans. Brace Jovanovich, in *Walter Benjamin: Selected Writings* (Cambridge, MA: Harvard University Press, 1996), pp. 236–52.

2 https://bit.ly/3SRn1pg (last accessed 21 February 2024).

3 BVerfG, Judgement on 26 May 1993, AZ 1 BvR 208/93.

4 Immanuel Kant, *Groundwork of the Metaphysics of Morals*, trans. and ed. Mary Gregor (Cambridge: Cambridge University Press, 1997), p. 37 (emphasis in the original).

5 Edward J. Eberle, 'The German Idea of Freedom' (2008) **10** *Oregon Review of International Law* 1–76.

6 www.gesetze-im-internet.de/englisch_gg/englisch_gg .html#p0023 (last accessed 1 July 2023).

7 Edward J. Eberle, 'Observations on the Development of Human Dignity and Personality in German Constitutional Law: An Overview' (2012) **33** *Liverpool Law Review* 201–33, 211.

8 Alex Tuckness, 'Locke's Political Philosophy' in Edward N. Zalta and Uri Nodelman (eds), *The Stanford Encyclopedia of Philosophy*, Fall 2023 ed.; see also C. B. Macpherson, *The Political Theory of Possessive Individualism: Hobbes to Locke* (Oxford: Clarendon Press, 1962).

9   BVerfG, Judgement on 26 May 1993, AZ 1 BvR 208/93.
10 Ibid.
11 For an excellent analysis of shock therapy as a neoliberal strategy of governance, see: Naomi Klein, *The Shock Doctrine: The Rise of Disaster Capitalism* (New York: Picador, 2008).
12 Maria Jarosz, *Wygrani i przegrani polskiej transformacji* (Warsaw: Oficyna Naukowa, 2005).
13 Hannah Arendt, '8. Public Rights and Private Interests: In Response to Charles Frankel' in M. Mooney and F. Stuber (eds), *Small Comforts for Hard Times* (New York: Columbia University Press, 1977), p. 108.
14 Marc Galanter, 'Why the "Haves" Come Out Ahead: Speculations on the Limits of Legal Change' (1974) 9(1) *Law & Society Review* 95–160.
15 These are: Berliner MieterVerein e.V., Berliner MieterGemeinschaft e.V. and Mieterschutzbund.
16 The singing of the Cottbusser Choir is documented in a movie titled *Miete essen Seele auf* [Rent Eats the Soul], dir. Angelika Levi, 2016.
17 Deutsche Wohhnen SE, company presentation (power point slides), 2017.
18 Christoph Trautvetter, *Who Owns the City? Analysis of Property Owner Groups and Their Business Practices on the Berlin Real Estate Market* (Berlin: Rosa Luxemburg Stiftung, 2020).
19 Adolf A. Berle and Gardiner C. Means, *The Modern Corporation and Private Property* (New York: Harcourt, Brace & World, 1968 [1932]), p. 18.
20 Jean-Philippe Robé, *Property, Power and Politics: Why We Need to Rethink the World Power System* (Bristol: Bristol University Press, 2020), p. 231.
21 Directive 2007/36/EC of the European Parliament and of the Council of 11 July 2007 on the exercise of certain rights of shareholders in listed companies. See also: Lynn A. Stout, *The Shareholder Value Myth: How Putting Shareholders First Harms Investors, Corporations, and the Public* (San Francisco, CA: Berrett-Koehler, 2012).

[22] Berle and Means, *The Modern Corporation and Private Property*, note 19 above.

[23] https://bit.ly/49AQLOc (last accessed 21 February 2024).

[24] Joel Bakan, *The Corporation: The Pathological Pursuit of Profit and Power*, Free Press trade paperback ed. (New York: Free Press, 2005), pp. 61ff.

[25] This is the Qatari Investment Authority. See: www.bbc.com/news/business-40192970 (last accessed 21 February 2024).

[26] Saskia Sassen, 'The Politics of Equity: Who Owns the City?' Lecture at the London School of Economics, 25 November 2015, www.youtube.com/watch?v=UAQuyizBIug (last accessed 21 February 2024).

[27] https://bit.ly/3T7hImR (last accessed 21 February 2024).

[28] *Stadt als Beute*, directed by Andreas Wilcke, 2015.

[29] A 1993 law (*Altschuldenhilfegesetz*) obliged East German municipalities to privatise at least 15 per cent of their housing stock.

[30] Benedict Ugarte Chacón, *Berlin Bank Skandal: eine Studie zu den Vorgängen um die Bankgesellschaft Berlin*, 1st ed. (Münster: Westfälisches Dampfboot, 2012).

[31] Philipp P. Metzger, *Die Finanzialisierung der deutschen Ökonomie am Beispiel des Wohnungsmarktes*, 1st ed. (Münster: Westfälisches Dampfboot, 2020).

[32] https://de.marketscreener.com/kurs/aktie/DEUTSCHE-WOHNEN-SE-487040/unternehmen/ (last accessed 21 February 2024).

[33] See e.g.: Katharina Pistor, *The Code of Capital: How the Law Creates Wealth and Inequality* (Princeton, NJ: Princeton University Press, 2019).

[34] https://bit.ly/3UOhJ0w (last accessed 1 September 2023).

[35] Hartwig Dieser, 'Restitution. Wie funktioniert sie und was bewirkt sie?' in Hartmut Häußermann and Reiner Reef (eds), *Stadtentwicklung in Ostdeutschland* (Opladen: Westdeutscher Verlag, 1996), pp. 129–38.

[36] 'Fehl-Steuer Ost', *Der Spiegel*, 46/1997, 32–48.

[37] Matthias Bernt and Andrej Holm, 'Die Ostdeutschlandforschung muss das Wohnen in den Blick nehmen: Plädoyer für eine neue politisch-institutionelle

Perspektive auf ostdeutsche Städte' (2020) **8** *sub\urban. zeitschrift für kritische stadtforschung* 97–114.

Chapter 3

1 https://bit.ly/3ORiTV8 (last accessed 21 February 2024).
2 https://taz.de/Initiative-Neue-Wege-fuer-Berlin/!5649089/ (last accessed 21 February 2024).
3 Friedrich Engels and Karl Marx, *The Communist Manifesto* (London: Penguin Classics, 2015).
4 Fabian Thiel, 'Artikel 15 GG – obsolet? Helmut Ridder zum 100. Geburtstag' (2019) **13** *Die Öffentliche Verwaltung* 497–507.
5 The summary of the discussion can be found at: https://bit.ly/3I524SZ (last accessed 21 February 2024).
6 https://bit.ly/42KAHHn (last accessed 21 February 2024).
7 A lawyer involved in legislating the *Mietendeckel*, interviewed by Joanna Kusiak in Berlin on 19 September 2019.
8 Gutachten zur rechtlichen Bewertung der Forderungen der Initiative Deutsche Wohnen & Co. enteignen, Wissenschaftlicher Parlamentsdienst, Berlin, 21 August 2019.
9 https://taz.de/DW-Enteignen-fordert-Geisel-Ruecktritt/!5882439/ (last accessed 21 February 2024).
10 https://bit.ly/3OT49VX (last accessed 21 February 2024).
11 Gunther Teubner explains it well with the metaphor of the twelfth camel. Cf. Gunther Teubner, 'Alienating Justice: On the Surplus Value of the Twelfth Camel' in Jiří Přibáň and David Nelken (eds), *Law's New Boundaries: Consequences of Legal Autopoiesis* (Aldershot: Ashgate, 2001), pp. 21–44.
12 Eric Voegelin, 'Descent into the Legal Abyss' in *Hitler and the Germans: The Collected Works of Eric Voegelin* (Baton Rouge, LA: Louisiana State University Press, 1989), Vol. 31, trans. and ed. by D. Clemens and B. Purcell.
13 Gunther Teubner, *Law as an Autopoietic System* (Oxford: Blackwell, 1993).
14 Pistor, *The Code of Capital*, note 33 above (Chapter 2); see also this brief video which explains it well: https://bit.ly/3UOZ4Bt (last accessed 21 February 2024).

15 Amy Kapczynski, 'Partisan Warriors and Political Courts', https://lpeproject.org/blog/partisan-warriors-and-political-courts/ (last accessed 21 February 2024).

16 Joanna Kusiak, *Chaos Warszawa. Porządki przestrzenne polskiego kapitalizmu* [Chaos Warsaw: The spatial orders of Polish capitalism] (Warsaw: Bęc Zmiana, 2017).

17 Grzegorz Piątek, *Najlepsze miasto świata: Warszawa w odbudowie 1944–1949* [The best city in the world: Warsaw in reconstruction 1944–1949] (Warsaw: WAB, 2020).

18 Joanna Kusiak, 'Rule of Law and Rules-Lawyering: Legal Corruption and "Reprivatization Business" in Warsaw' (2019) **43**(3) *International Journal of Urban and Regional Research* 589–96, 593.

19 Ibid., pp. 589–96.

20 Carl Jung, *Collected Works* (Princeton, NJ: Princeton University Press, 1966), Vol. 16, p. 65.

21 Audre Lorde, 'The Uses of Anger' in *Sister Outsider: Essays and Speeches* (Berkeley, CA: Crossing Press, 2007), p. 127.

22 John L. Hammond, 'Mística, meaning and popular education in the Brazilian Landless Workers Movement' (2014) **6**(1) *Interface: A Journal for and About Social Movements* 372–91.

23 Pistor, *The Code of Capital*, note 33 above (Chapter 2); T. Piketty, *Capital in the Twenty-First Century* (Cambridge, MA: Belknap Press of Harvard University Press, 2014).

Chapter 4

1 Heike Drummer, Jutta Zwilling and Hessische Landesregierung (Hrsg.) (eds), *'Ein Glücksfall für die Demokratie': Elisabeth Selbert (1896–1986); die große Anwältin der Gleichberechtigung* (Frankfurt: Eichborn, 1999).

2 Heribert Prantl, Ein Liebeskummer-Brief, *Süddeutsche Zeitung*, 16 May 2014.

3 Ibid.

4 www.fluter.de/sites/default/files/recht_so.pdf (last accessed 21 February 2024).

5 https://bit.ly/48ssd90 (last accessed 21 February 2024).

6 Ibid.

7 Ibid.

8 This fragment is based on: Adam Tooze, *The Wages of Destruction: The Making and Breaking of the Nazi Economy* (New York: Penguin USA, 2008), pp. 99–106.

9 Hoffrogge, 'Nie wirklich weg', note 2 above (Chapter 1).

10 The so-called Ahlen Programm of the CDU. Quoted from ibid.

11 The text of Article 15, translated here by the author. The official translation of the *Grundgesetz* into English, provided by the Ministry of Justice, only reflects that, for a long time, the concept of *Vergesellschaftung* was forgotten or misunderstood even by official bodies. The translators mistakenly translated *Vergesellschaftung* as 'nationalisation' (which would be *Verstaatlichung*). While nationalisation simply transfers property to the state, socialised property can be owned by public bodies, cooperatives or even private individuals, as long as it is subject to democratic control.

12 Expertenkommission zum Volksentscheid, Vergesellschaftung großer Wohnungsunternehmen. Abschlussbericht, June 2023, p. 37, www.berlin.de/ kommission-vergesellschaftung/downloads/.

13 Clara Maier, 'The Weimar Origins of the West German Rechtsstaat, 1919–1969' (2019) **62**(4) *The Historical Journal* 1069–91, 1077.

14 Peter Caldwell, 'Rights, Citizenship, and Society: The Social Rechtsstaat' in *Democracy, Capitalism, and the Welfare State*, (Oxford: Oxford University Press, 2019), pp. 45–70.

15 Peter Caldwell, 'Ernst Forsthoff and the Legacy of Radical Conservative State Theory in the Federal Republic of Germany' (winter 1994) **15**(4) *History of Political Thought* 615–41.

16 Ernst Forsthoff, *Der totale Staat*, quoted from: https://bit.ly/ 3uHAc43 (last accessed 21 February 2024).

17 www.wiltonpark.org.uk/about-us/history-of-wilton-park/ (last accessed 21 February 2024).

18 Quoted in: Helga Grebing, *Konservative gegen die Demokratie. Konservative Kritik an der Demokratie in der Bundesrepublik nach 1945* (Frankfurt: Europäische Verlagsanstalt, 1971), p. 383.

[19] Florian Meinel, *Der Jurist in der industriellen Gesellschaft. Ernst Forsthoff und seine Zeit* (Berlin: Akademie Verlag, 2011), p. 226.

[20] Caldwell, 'Ernst Forsthoff', note 15 above, p. 629.

[21] BVerfE 5, 85.

[22] Wolfgang Abendroth, 'Um den Sozialisierungsartikel des Grundgesetzes' in Michael Buckmiller (ed.), *Wolfgang Abendroth. Gesammelte Schriften*, Vol. 3: 1956–1963 (Hannover: Offizin Verlag, 2013), p. 177.

[23] 'The Programme of Solidarność', translated into English by the editorial collective of *Labour Focus on Eastern Europe: A Socialist Defence Bulletin on Eastern Europe and the USSR*, Vol. 5, Nos 1–2 (spring 1982), p. 4.

[24] Jarosław Kuisz, *Charakter prawny porozumień sierpniowych 1980–1981* (Warsaw: Trio, 2009).

[25] 'The Programme of Solidarność', note 23 above, p. 3.

[26] Jacek Tittenbrun, *The Collapse of Real Socialism in Poland* (London: Janus Publishing, 1993), p. 15.

[27] Klein, *The Shock Doctrine*, note 11 above (Chapter 2), p. 175.

[28] Tadeusz Kowalik, *From Solidarity to Sellout: The Restoration of Capitalism in Poland* (New York: Monthly Review Press, 2012).

[29] Leslie Wayne, 'A Doctor for Struggling Economies', *The New York Times*, 1 October 1989, p. 1.

[30] Mitchell A. Orenstein, *Out of the Red: Building Capitalism and Democracy in Postcommunist Europe* (Ann Arbor, MI: University of Michigan Press, 2001), p. 25.

[31] Jacek Tittenbrun and Przemysław Pluciński, 'Pod wiatr historii. O polskiej transformacji, prywatyzacji i przegranych alternatywach' (2015) 4(110) *Le Monde Diplomatique, Edycja Polska* 6–10.

[32] David Ost, *The Defeat of Solidarity: Anger and Politics in Postcommunist Europe*, 1st print, Cornell paperbacks ed. (Ithaca, NY: Cornell University Press, 2006).

[33] https://bit.ly/3UPP2QL (last accessed 21 February 2024).

[34] https://bit.ly/48QoHFK (last accessed 21 February 2024).

[35] Peter Mair, *Ruling the Void: The Hollowing of Western Democracy* (London: Verso, 2013).

[36] Ibid.

[37] Wolfgang Streeck, *How Will Capitalism End? Essays on a Failing System* (London: Verso, 2016), p. 53.

[38] Elinor Ostrom, *Governing the Commons: The Evolution of Institutions for Collective Action* (Cambridge and New York: Cambridge University Press, 2015).

[39] https://bit.ly/3wPqVrf (last accessed 21 February 2024).

[40] Jurgen Habermas, *The Theory of Communicative Action: A Critique of Functionalist Reason*, trans. by T. McCarthy (Boston, MA: Beacon Press, 1987), Vol. 2, p. 264.

[41] Wendy Brown, *Undoing the Demos: Neoliberalism's Stealth Revolution*, 1st ed. (New York: Zone Books, 2015), pp. 151ff.

[42] Walter Benjamin, 'On the Concept of History' in *Walter Benjamin: Selected Writings*, Vol. 4: 1938–1940 ed. by Howard Eiland and Michael W. Jennings (Cambridge, MA: Harvard University Press, 2006).

[43] Moody's Investors Service. Issuer Comment: Land of Berlin. Proposed referendum to expropriate multi-unit private properties would cost Berlin up to €36 billion, a credit negative, 8 March 2019.

Chapter 5

[1] Winfred Brenne and Deutscher Werkbund Berlin (eds), *Bruno Taut: Master of Colourful Architecture in Berlin* (Salenstein: Braun Publishing, 2013), p. 11.

[2] Paul L. Knox, *Palimpsests: Biographies of 50 City Districts. International Case Studies for Urban Change* (Basel: Birkhäuser, 2012), p. 120.

[3] Anne Kockelkorn, 'Financialized Berlin: The Monetary Transformation of Housing, Architecture and Polity' (2022) **26** *Architectural Theory Review* 76–104.

[4] Ibid.

[5] Deutsche Wohnen & Co. enteignen has calculated this by dividing the €972 million that Vonovia paid out in shareholders' dividends in 2020 by the 415,688 rental apartments it owned that year. This results in a dividend contribution of €2,300 per apartment per year.

[6] Vonovia Remuneration Report 2022, p. 25, www.vonovia
.com/en/investors/corporate-governance/compensation (last
accessed 22 February 2024).

[7] Brenne and Deutscher Werkbund Berlin, *Bruno Taut*, note 1
above, p. 11.

[8] https://bit.ly/49C2Kv2 (last accessed 21 February 2024).

[9] Karl-Heinz Peters, *Von der Gemeinnützigkeit zum Profit:
Privatisierungsopfer Gehag – Herausforderung für alternative
Wohnungspolitik* (Hamburg: VSA Verlag, 2016), pp. 41–8.

[10] Ibid., p. 68.

[11] Paul Ulrich, 'Neubau rechnet sich nicht', *Berliner Zeitung*, 29
December 2010.

[12] The overall vision of the AöR's institutional design, as
presented in this chapter, is based on the details worked out
by Deutsche Wohnen & Co. enteignen. The vision of the
democratic decision-making process, based on the
procedures used in mediation and conflict resolution, is my
creative addition to the movement's future vision. For the
institutional design of the AöR, see: 'Deutsche Wohnen & Co.
enteignen, Gemeingut Wohnen: Eine Anstalt des
öffentlichen Rechts für Berlins vergesellschaftete
Wohnungsbestände' (Berlin: DWE, 2023).

[13] Article 14, GG.

[14] BVerfGE 24, 367.

[15] www.youtube.com/watch?v=oijmRknMXOI (last accessed
6 March 2024).

[16] I thank Kalle Kunkel for inspiring this fragment.

* Note that section 7 of Chapter 5 weaves in real quotes from
Albert Einstein, Walter Benjamin and Tim Burton's 2010 movie
Alice in Wonderland.

Chapter 6

[1] www.youtube.com/watch?v=FXj-695FEHw (last accessed 22
February 2024).

[2] Josh Cohen, 'The Politics of Anger: Putin and the Psychology
of Rage' (2022), **110** *The Yale Review* 57–68.

3   Jonathan Haidt (ed.), *The Righteous Mind: Why Good People Are Divided by Politics and Religion*, Vintage Books ed. (New York: Vintage Books, 2013).

4   Marcus Böick, 'In from the Socialist "Cold", but Burned by the Capitalist "Heat"? The Dynamics of Political Revolution and Economic Transformation in Eastern Germany after 1990' (2020) **16** *Sustainability: Science, Practice and Policy* 143–54.

5   Gunther Teubner, 'Exogenous Self-Binding: How Social Subsystems Externalise Their Foundational Paradoxes in the Process of Constitutionalisation' in Gunther Teubner (ed.), *Critical Theory and Legal Autopoiesis: The Case for Societal Constitutionalism* (Manchester: Manchester University Press, 2019), pp. 319–20.

6   Christoph Menke, 'Law and Violence' in Alessandro Ferrara and Christoph Menke (eds), *Law and Violence: Christoph Menke in Dialogue* (Manchester: Manchester University Press, 2018), p. 3.

7   Walter Benjamin, 'Critique of Violence' in *Walter Benjamin: Selected Writings*, Vol. 1: 1913–1926, ed. by Marcus Bullock and Michael Jennings (Cambridge, MA: Harvard University Press, 1996).

8   Jedediah Britton-Purdy, 'No Law Without Politics (No Politics Without Law)', 2018, https://lpeproject.org/blog/no-law-without-politics-no-politics-without-law/ (last accessed 22 February 2024).

9   Zoe Adams, *Labour and the Wage: A Critical Perspective* (New York: Oxford University Press, 2020).

10 E. P. Thompson, *Whigs and Hunters: The Origin of the Black Act* (New York: Pantheon Books, 1975).

11 Andreas Philippopoulos-Mihalopoulos, 'The Foundational Paradox of Gunther Teubner' in Teubner, *Critical Theory and Legal Autopoiesis*, note 5 above, p. 3.

12 Ibid.

13 Anne Dailey, 'Why Psychoanalysis Matters to Law' in *Law and the Unconscious: A Psychoanalyic Perspective* (New Haven, CT: Yale University Press, 2017).

[14] Rolf Reber, *Critical Feeling: How to Use Feelings Strategically* (Cambridge: Cambridge University Press, 2016).

[15] Olga Tokarczuk, '*The Tender Narrator: Nobel Lecture by Olga Tokarczuk* (Stockholm: Svenska Akademien, 2018).

[16] Edgar H. Schein, 'Kurt Lewin's Change Theory in the Field and in the Classroom: Notes Toward a Model of Managed Learning' (1996) 9(1) *Systems Practice* 27–47, 34.

[17] Interview with Peter's colleague, conducted via Zoom on 23 November 2023.

Chapter 7

[1] This epilogue story is a rewrite of: Franz Kafka, 'Before the Law', translated by M. Hoffman, in *Metamorphosis and Other Stories* (London: Penguin Books, 2008), pp. 197–8.

Soundtrack

[1] Check on YouTube at: www.youtube.com/watch?v= 1udi3OIuriA (last accessed 11 April 2024).

Printed in the United States
by Baker & Taylor Publisher Services